Stop Pitching & Start Connecting

Social Media Strategies for Network Marketing and Direct Sales

By Alex Theis

To Stacie, Courtney, Patrick, Travis, and Kaylie – my fabulous family.

Table of Contents

INTRODUCTION

Social media is here to stay and growing like crazy every day. Smart phones have made the phenomenon grow at an even faster pace. People can post on Facebook, put a picture on Instagram, or send a tweet from almost anywhere using their phone.

Like any undertaking, building a platform on social media, developing your personal brand, or heck, even just opening a Twitter account, can seem like a big deal. It is. But it should not be intimidating. It should be fun, rewarding, and an extension of who you are.

It's time for network marketers to be prepared and confident. Social media is the ultimate word-of-mouth vehicle. Network marketing is built on the best advertising in the world – **word-of-mouth** advertising. The two were made to work together. Yet, as a whole, the network marketing community has yet to seize this golden opportunity. The success of network marketers will depend on their ability to maximize social media and digital marketing, build their personal brand, connect with people, and attract social networkers.

This means the future of *your* business will revolve heavily around social media and your ability to use it effectively.

I'm sick and tired of seeing networkers struggle with social media. Lack of social media savvy doesn't have to hold you back. The benefits of effectively using social media far outweigh any potential negatives. There's no reason to keep putting off discovering the effective use of this powerful tool. You've learned many new things in your life. How to walk. How to ride a bike. How to drive a car. How to use a mobile phone, email, and the World Wide Web. Social media is no different. It takes time, determination, practice, education, and an open mind.

Social networking is packed full of professional people, entrepreneurs, thought leaders, and people just waiting to meet you. It is not a hangout for the socially inept or a place to waste precious time. Social media makes it easier than ever to connect with like-minded people. It can lead to in-person meetings and connections. And isn't that what we're looking for? Great businesses are built on a foundation of teamwork and strong leaders who align with people who think like they do and want more out of life.

Time is one of the most precious gifts we have. It is more valuable than money and cannot be replaced. I hate it when people waste my time or yours. This book will not waste your time, I promise. Instead it offers strategies for engaging with social media in ways that are effective and efficient.

Very few things make me happier than helping people get what they want. I've built a career based on my mission in life – helping people see they can go for their dreams and giving them simple actions steps toward achieving those dreams. As a network marketer you are already in a class of your own. I love entrepreneurs because you view things in a different way. There's something you want in life, and you see your business as a path to get it. Kudos to you for being a forward thinker and entrepreneur. The world needs more people like you to help others take their dreams off the shelf and take steps towards making them a reality.

Social media is here to stay. Digital marketing is thriving. Why not master it in your own unique way? It's a wide open opportunity, just waiting for you to take hold of the flame.

Ready to get started? Good. Let's roll!

PART I: YOUR SOCIAL MEDIA MINDSET

SECTION 1: WHY USE SOCIAL MEDIA?

Something was amiss. My wife didn't put on a skirt. She didn't do her hair. Why wasn't she getting ready for work?

"What's going on?" I asked.

Tears welled in her brown eyes. "I'm not going back to work. I'm staying home with our son."

What was she thinking, quitting? Panic wrapped me like a cold, wet blanket as questions sped through my head like runaway train cars. She made twice what I did. Had the job with the excellent benefits. We wouldn't survive. Why couldn't she just go back to work like other women did when their maternity leave ended?

When my first son was born I was so excited I couldn't speak. Every time I tried to tell someone about little Patrick, emotion knotted my throat and made me cry.

But I never expected this. "Stacie—"

"I can't take Patrick to daycare," she continued.

"I'll drive him." I wasn't proud of the pleading tremble in my voice. "Just try it, Stacie."

She didn't budge. "Everything will be all right."

How could she stay so calm?

"This is all part of God's plan for our lives."

"You know my salary won't cut it." Sure I'd been in a career rut for a while, but I'd thought Stacie's great job meant I had time to figure it out. We'd have to move in with her parents. The panic morphed into feelings of inadequacy, failure, and shame.

"Don't worry." Her soothing voice disarmed me. "I believe in you. Something good will happen." Stacie's words pierced my heart. No amount of pleading, begging, or reasoning would change this decision. Her mind was made up. Not out of stubbornness, but out of faith for the future.

Patrick is now seventeen. We survived not only his baby years, but those of his siblings, and I understand now what Stacie was saying back then. She was asking me not to worry about how it would come together. She wanted me to focus on the bigger picture.

Our 'why' for making that decision was far greater than any 'how'.

Stacie wanted me to trust that the end result would be great. Her faith was unwavering. She truly believed what she was saying.

While I was scared, I trusted her. I trusted that God indeed had something bigger in store for me.

It's funny the way belief, faith, and trust can put forces in motion that you cannot see or predict. By focusing on the 'why' and by rowing the boat forward every single day, people become activated to help you. People you've never met or people you would least expect to help you get ahead will see strength in your confidence.

My son was born October 17, 1997. My wife was supposed to go back to work on December 1. The very next week I received a call I didn't expect and couldn't believe. It was a friend who was working with a new, growing company. He said they needed help right away.

On December 17, I started the job. I made more money with great benefits. Just as important, the job was nearly a perfect fit for me. It was in an industry that would profoundly impact my life: **network marketing**.

My wife's decision to stay home altered the course of our lives forever. It was her belief that put magical forces into action. She's been home with our children, and I've been involved in network marketing since that important day.

We all need someone to believe in us. We also need to have faith in our abilities and know our 'why'. The 'how' becomes diminished when we have a strong enough reason to accomplish something.

I believe in you. If you will trust this process, have faith in your abilities, and keep your 'why' strong, I believe good things are going to happen.

We all need encouragement and instruction in life. You may have struggled learning to use social media. You may have started a blog and stopped it before it gained momentum. Maybe you tried Twitter but you just didn't get it.

I wrote this book because I believe the right people will read it. The right people will put it into action. The right people will use the strategies to impact more lives than I could ever reach. YOU are one of those right people!

You have a story. You have a purpose. You have a calling. Whatever it is, I want to help you use social networking in a powerful way to help your dreams come true.

Just like Stacie's belief, faith, and 'why' put invisible forces in motion, I believe you can do the same thing. Using social media, you will find people who have been waiting to meet you their entire lives.

There are a lot of reasons to use social media, like increasing your warm market or establishing credibility in your circles. But before we dive in, pause a moment and think about *your* biggest "why." What drives you to go after your dreams and goals? Using social media is simply one more tool to help you reach your big goals, but it is NOT the primary why.

Learning effective social network marketing is a *how*, but it is not the only how. You are already doing other things to build your business. Social media supports these things; it does not stand alone. While social media is like a golden key to unlock new opportunities, used in isolation it will not build your dreams.

Now that we've cleared that up, let's examine one of those important smaller whys, the why behind the choice to learn social media. Let me be very clear about what it is not. It is not to sell or pitch. Instead, it is all about connection. *Stop Pitching and Start Connecting* is not a theory, it's a proven strategy. From fitness and health experts to network marketing executives, to life coaches and full-time bloggers, the goal of those who engage successfully in social network marketing is to genuinely connect with people. As they kept this important "why" at the forefront of their social media goals, they found success. You can too.

You have what it takes, I promise. I'll help you fill in the blanks and missing pieces with the smaller "whys" and practical application. As we move forward, trust the process, focus on the BIG why and not the how, and believe this is going to work for you in ways you could never imagine.

Now let's start creating some magic!

CHAPTER 1: WHY USE SOCIAL MEDIA

"Social media is so perfect for our industry. Anytime you can connect two people together and you have a message that resonates, I think you're going to be able to do some amazing things. If you don't have a message that resonates, it doesn't matter what social media does, you're going nowhere fast. You need a good message, a good presence, and a good strategy. That's a combination for great things to happen." –BK Boreyko, who has over 20 years of experience as both a distributor and an owner of the multi-million dollar companies he founded in the in the wellness and network marketing industries.

Because you're reading this, you must realize that social media, also referred to as social networking, is here to stay in a big way. You're ready to take action and start using it to your advantage. But maybe you're on the fence or maybe you need validation for making the decision to read this.

Allow me to make you feel good about why you've made a great choice and why you need to start using social media consistently and effectively.

The 97%

In Chet Holmes' book *The Ultimate Sales Machine*, he refers to a 'buying pyramid' that goes like this:

- 3% of people are looking for what you have.
- 7% are open to buying, but not currently looking
- 30% not currently in the market, but could be in the future
- 30% think they're not interested
- 30% know they're not interested and may never be

There are different ways to look at this, but here's what I want you to take away: How can you reach the 97% of people who are not currently looking for what you have? How can you get them in your pipeline?

We want to focus on the 3% already interested, absolutely. But when you're focused on such a small number, it can seem daunting. What are ways you can get the other 97%, or even the 37% who might become interested, into your marketing/sales/prospecting funnel?

One terrific answer (bonus points if you got it on your first guess): Social media

Social media is loaded with people you can get into your funnel WITHOUT pitching them or presenting to them. You see, pitching or selling them will NOT work. They're not interested right now. Using social media to pitch or sell will only chase away the 97% you want to reach. The trick, as great marketing people know, is to create a brand and presence to get people into your fan club so that when they're ready, YOU are their trusted source.

You are no doubt going to spend a lot of your time prospecting for the 3%. That's smart. But why not maximize your time and leverage social media to reach the other 97%?

Be one of the few

Another reason to use social media and focus on the 97%: most people won't. You read that right. Most people will struggle and press and exhaust themselves on the 3% and NEVER go after the 97% or even the 7% who are open to what you have to offer.

In addition, most people will NOT take the time to learn social media and all of its tools because they don't see the instant results, the instant gratification many people look for constantly.

By learning how to use social media correctly, being consistent, adding value to others, putting out great content, and connecting instead of pitching, you will be one of the few who actually follow through. The world is full of good ideas and intentions, but very few people take it from concept to execution.

For me, the easiest analogy for this is book writing. We all have at least one book in us and there are varying stats that show that 80-95% of us have a desire to write a book. But how many people will actually follow through and write that book? Less than 1%.

Stand out, be unique, and create a competitive advantage for yourself in network marketing by being one of the few to harness the power of social media through connecting, not pitching.

12 exposures

Another great sales graph I learned over the years goes something like this:

Percent of sales that occur after each exposure: One exposure, 2%; two exposures, 3%; three exposures, 5%; four exposures, 10%; five or more exposures, 80%.

By contrast, people stop following up after: One exposure, 44%; two exposures, 66%; three exposures, 82%; four exposures, 92%; ONLY 8% or less follow up past four exposures!!!

These stats, which ring true for every direct sales opportunity I've been associated with (it's still about sales), suggest that if you put 100 networkers in a room, only eight of them would follow up with someone five or more times. That means only eight people would do what it takes to get 80% of the sales or partnerships they seek.

You see, follow up does NOT have to be presenting or selling every time. It can be subtle. It can be passive. Make it about them. It can be about anything but business, as long as it's genuine. It's called relationship building, and it's the foundation of great network marketing businesses.

With social media, you can reach more people than ever before. Utilize it to help follow up the number of times it will take to land great business partners and incredible customers.

Personal branding

I will go into this in depth in a later chapter because your personal brand is everything, and it begs your attention. For now, just know that social networking has made it easier and more rewarding than ever to develop a strong personal brand. We are all experts at something, and with social networking you can maximize your expertise and turn it into profitable relationships and business opportunities.

Numbers don't lie

Think social media is a fad or believe you will be fine without using it? Think you will get by doing only face to face or phone networking? Need some more edification that you made a great decision to read this book? Well, allow me to oblige.[1]

- 89% of people ages 18-29 use social media
- 78% of people ages 30-49 use social media
- 60% of people ages 50-64 use social media
- The fastest growing age demographic on Twitter is the 50-64 age bracket
- Social networking sites are increasingly used to keep up with social ties
- The average user of a social networking site is half as likely to be socially isolated as the average American
- Facebook users are more trusting than others and have more close relationships

The like-minded

Great network marketing leaders partner with the like-minded. This is one of the most important concepts to grasp in network marketing. And where can you find people who think like you, want the same things in life as you, and want to partner with you? Social media, guaranteed. Much of your success as a networker hinges on finding people who have similar tastes, opinions, thoughts, aspirations, morals, and beliefs. It does not mean they need to have the same skills, experiences, strengths, or personalities. Social media is like fishing in ponds you didn't know were there. It's like climbing a block wall and finding a city you never knew existed, full of people who want to connect with you.

It's one of the things I absolutely love about social media, especially Twitter and blogging – it has allowed me to connect with people I never would have met without it.

Thought leaders

If you want to live the life of your dreams, you have to spend time with the right people. Meeting and associating with people who have accomplished what you want to accomplish and who are living the type of life you are working toward is critical to your success. Connect with thought leaders and you are taking steps to become one.

Through social networking and digital marketing, you have instant access to thought leaders both within your industry and niche and outside these areas. These are people who have expertise in topics you are interested in (hopefully business, sales, personal development, increasing your network, marketing, etc.).

Connecting with them, following them, reading their blogs, listening to their podcasts, watching their videos, and observing their strategy is all virtually free and readily available. Watching how they interact with fans, customers, and prospects can be highly educational. Interacting and engaging with thought leaders elevates your associations, beliefs, and skills.

Throughout this book you will hear from people who have had success with YouTube, podcasting, written blogs, Twitter, Facebook, Pinterest, in-person networking, LinkedIn, and information products. They are speakers, business owners, coaches, authors, bloggers, leaders, business people, and successful entrepreneurs. All of them are in this book for a reason. They believed in the heart of this book, that social media has to be about genuine connection and a desire to make the world a better place through that connection. They believe in the power of entrepreneurs, social media, and network marketing.

Healthy social networking happens when we are 100% genuine and care about building genuine relationships. Being the genuine you is the only way to stake your claim and get results. As you learn from others, seek out those who share this value.

Driving traffic

"I want people to be drawn to me. I know that when I put out a tweet those words can be powerful. I want an authentic nature that draws people towards me. You have to be careful of selling and self-promoting. You don't have to be afraid to do it, but do it sparingly. That's my style, same as I would do at a social gathering. I want to ask enough questions so people ask me what I do." –Steve Gutzler, voted Most Inspirational Leader on Social Media by the readers of *The Huffington Post.* He is also the President of Leadership Quest and author of the book *Emotional Intelligence for Personal Leadership.*

So you have a website for your network marketing business. How do you drive traffic to it? Your business card? Great search engine optimization (SEO)? Internet and pay per click advertising?

It's easy to get lost in the world of getting to the top of Google searches, creating ads and writing copy, spending money on internet advertising, and perfecting your SEO. But with social media, you can get ahead of the game by spending just a little bit of time each week implanting a solid strategy.

You start a blog and post solid, useful content regularly. You also post great content on Twitter, Facebook, or Pinterest. Some of these posts tell people about your blog. People start reading and subscribing to your blog. You start building a contact list. You promote other people, their blogs, and their businesses on social media. They like what you're up to and start promoting your blog. Your blog includes a YouTube video or audio podcast once a month. This drives traffic to your site.

With consistency and a focus on connecting, not selling, you organically build a virtual fan club of people who promote you, read your content, and connect with you. Do you see how you can start reaching the 97%? Understand how you can passively create exposures and put yourself in position to get people in your sales funnel and grow your warm market daily?

It works. There are normal, common people like you and me who are doing this every day. They are using social media tools – posts, pictures, videos, audio, and their writing – to build an amazing platform which attracts thousands of like-minded people.

You can do this. It doesn't take amazing talent, great writing skills, or a lot of cash. It takes consistency and a long term approach. Are you willing to do the little things over and over that unsuccessful people aren't willing to do?

One of my greatest mentors, Peter Reilly, who now runs one of the largest bottling, canning, and manufacturing companies in the Southwestern United States, told me something that will stick with me forever. He said, "It's not the smartest guy with the best idea who gets ahead. It's the guy who is willing to work his butt off to make it happen."

Promoting events

"The days of, 'I didn't know that event was going on' are gone. It comes down to communication: letting people know and getting people on the same page. Like my dad used to say, 'The one who communicates the best, wins.' Social media helps you to be able to connect with people," according to BK Boreyko.

Event promotion alone might be a good enough reason to tap into the power of social networking. Reaching your team and target market has never been easier. Facebook even has an 'Events' feature to help you keep meetings on the radar.

Instant availability

Smartphone usage is increasing daily - 86% of smartphone users reported using their phone to make real-time queries to help them meet friends or solve problems.[2]

To build a great income in network marketing you have to build a great team. Great teams require constant, effective communication. Social media is real time and accessible from almost everywhere in the world via your smartphone.

Facebook is a great community tool to keep in touch, organize events, and recognize people. Twitter can be used as an all-inclusive chat room, an immediate news gathering or reporting site, and a place to widen your funnel. Instagram allows you to visually communicate with images and pictures. Pinterest gives you the ability to tap into a diverse market and organically introduce your products through recipes, infographics, and images.

The ultimate word-of-mouth machine

Network marketing is built on word of mouth. Word-of-mouth advertising is the most powerful advertising in the world. Trusted recommendations move more products, grow more sales, and get more people jobs and opportunities than any other form of advertising or marketing. It's who you know that matters, much more than what you know. You understand this because you're a networker.

Social media is the ultimate word-of-mouth machine. Think about it. It's all about connections, recommendations, and who you know. These two forces were meant to work together, in a big way. It's one of the best ways to reach new people.

Lydia Aswolf-Carey, book reviewer, blogger, and social media brand manager, says, "At first, only a few of my clients were business owners, but that number soon started to swell thanks to word of mouth," she said. "I have never needed to advertise in the traditional sense. All of my clients come from word of mouth or social media." Powerful stuff from someone who earns her livelihood from social media.

Social media is here to stay. The possibilities for connection are endless. It's your time to harness the power to create an online platform that attracts people like never before. If you follow through with this book, the application, and the strategies, you will develop a social media presence that you can be proud of. Like opening a surprise gift, you will look forward to each day because of the new and deeper connections you will build.

APPLICATION:

1. Decide right now that you will be one of the few who learns social media and sticks with it for the long haul. You and your business are worth it!
2. Within the next 24 hours, find three like-minded people or thought leaders you admire and check out their social media presence.
3. Start to create a list, in a notebook, journal, or electronic document, of what these leaders convey through their social media channels. Think about how you can relay who you are and what you stand for through social media, in a way that intrigues (never divisive).
4. Word of mouth can sometimes have a curious way of being reciprocal. Today, go out and promote someone or something you like on one social site. Do it genuinely, without any agenda or expecting anything in return. Promote to add value to others.

CHAPTER 2: SOCIAL MEDIA MYTHS AND OBJECTIONS

The last chapter gave solid reasons backed by solid data to help you buy-in to learning social media as part of your business plan. Maybe you're now fully on-board, but in case you have nagging questions, let's address the most common myths and objections to social media.

11 MYTHS AND OBJECTIONS

1. **MYTH: Social media just wastes time.**

Your sister-in-law (or fill in the blank of a relative, friend, or someone you know who spends all day posting memes and quotes on social media) might be a time waster on Facebook, but successful entrepreneurs and businesses will tell you it's not a waste of time. In fact, they will tell you it's essential to do business successfully today. Almost anything can be used as a time waster. Using social media well requires good time management.

2. **MYTH: Social media is for people who are social misfits.**

I was told something like this back in the late 1990's about the Internet. Many believed it was only used for chat rooms and adult material. Well, I think Amazon or Google would tell you differently. The same goes for social media. There are millions, if not billions of social, successful, optimistic people on social networking sites right now just waiting to meet you.

3. **OBJECTION: I've tried selling on social networks, it doesn't work.**

Okay, this IS true. Selling on social media doesn't work, at least if that's all you're trying to do. If all you do is pitch, pitch, pitch, you're actually chasing people away instead of attracting.

Steve Gutzler says, "The biggest mistake I see people making on social media? They are doing more harm than good, not to others, but to their own brand and purpose."

Later chapters will offer strategy that will inevitably lead to results (i.e. sales), so hang with me. But remember, the why behind social media is connecting, not pitching.

4. MYTH: It takes too much time.

Chris Freytag, national health and wellness expert, author, fitness personality and regular contributor to *Prevention* and *Success*, says "Budget your time - time manage your social media. I might go in once a day and spend 15 minutes to answer questions. I could spend that time watching TV, but I use it to connect with people."

Most people who use social media effectively maximize **time management.** I spend less than 30 minutes a day on social media. I often feel this is some of the best time I spend networking during the day. As a network marketer, if your time management stinks, you're not going to go far anyway, with or without social media. We'll learn how to make the most of our time on social media for the long haul.

"It takes a long term view. If you join a gym, don't expect results in first month. Just like your business, you get out of it what you put into it," says Jamie Stewart, Managing Director of Momentum Factor Europe Ltd., a full service social media management and strategy company. Jamie also engineered a turnaround as Managing Director of Kleeneze, one of the leading direct sales companies in the United Kingdom.

5. MYTH: Social media doesn't lead to in-person networking or real relationships.

Blatantly false. Social media is being used daily to drive in-person meetings, strengthen communication between existing business relationships, and forge new ones. Now, if you're looking at it as a dating mechanism, I have no idea what kind of results it will produce (although I do know someone who met their wife on Match.com). If you're looking to meet thought leaders and people you can connect with, who may be looking for what you have, social media WILL lead to real, genuine, mutually beneficial relationships, if you do it right.

6.   OBJECTION: I can't keep one site straight from another.

It can be overwhelming when you first start interacting with social media, but I'm not a proponent for engaging with every site out there. The answer to this quandary is simple: reduce the number of sites you use. I focus on one main social networking channel (Twitter) and use a few others that work for me. The trick is picking a site or sites that will work for you. Choosing your social media channels is a big part of this book (see – aren't you glad you're reading it now?).

7.   OBJECTION: I tried that for a little while, it didn't work.

There's truth to this objection if social media is tried for a "little while." Social networking is a marathon, not a sprint. Back to the Chet Holmes book *The Ultimate Sales Machine*. In it he uses the phrase "Pig-headed discipline and determination" over and over and over. This phrase applies to social media prowess and results as well. It takes disciple and determination over the long term.

"The only way for social media to work is to be consistent," states Luke Dancy, social media strategist, marketing brand manager, and founder of Social Mischief.

Luke helped take celebrity magician Criss Angel's social media following from small to millions of likes and followers. How did he do it? One word: **CONSISTENCY.** All caps because I'm yelling? YES! Social media is a long-term, marathon approach, not a sprint or even half marathon.

Many people tell me they tried Twitter for a month and it didn't work. They tried to create a business page on Facebook, and it didn't work. They wrote a blog three or four times and stopped because no one subscribed to it.

Reality check: The social media world doesn't like quitters or people who aren't in it for the long haul. They are waiting to see if you're going to stick around. No one wants to read a blog if it's going to disappear in two months or only be updated once in a blue moon. Your pending audience needs consistency from you.

If it didn't work, you chose the wrong channel, were inconsistent, posted poor content, or failed to engage in the conversation. Don't worry, I'm here to help you do it and do it well.

8. **MYTH: My prospects aren't on social media, or, using social media hasn't helped me find prospects.**

As chapter one showed we looking for that 97%. Our prospects, mentors, associates, and customers most definitely ARE on social media. You just need to find the right site(s) and use it properly. You can build a platform to meet the type of quality people who could make your business soar and make building a business fun on many levels.

Social networks are filled with people who love to promote others. Build the right relationships, do social media right, and you will get people singing your praises and helping you grow your business without expecting anything in return.

9. **OBJECTION: People on social media aren't ready to buy.**

This is somewhat true. In fact, everywhere you go and any site you use, you will be lucky if 3% are ready to buy what you have to offer. With social media, we're going fishing in the big pond, where 97% of people who aren't ready to buy right now are swimming and could be ready to buy anytime. Will you build the connections needed to reel in the big fish when it's time?

10. **OBJECTION AND MYTH: I don't have anything to say.**

Nonsense. You are unique and you do have something to say. You have qualities that people are looking for.

I believe there is a self-esteem epidemic in the world, and it causes people to fall short of their potential or worse, never even try to reach it. They create objections and obstacles in their own head long before they ever surface in the real world, causing them to procrastinate, fail to take action, or settle for a life that's unfulfilling.

You have something to say. You just need help learning to use social media to reach your intended audience, people who will soak it up like a sponge.

11. OBJECTION: My personal life isn't for display – social media compromises my privacy.

We've all heard the horror stories of homes getting burglarized because people announced on Facebook that they were out of the country or on vacation, leading thieves straight to the loot. Yes, that can happen – if you're stupid about it.

News flash – you get to choose what you post on social media. You don't have to check in everywhere you go or tell everyone your personal plans, vacation dates, or post pictures of your kids, ages, or names. You can use social media as a business professional.

12. MYTH: Twitter is just for celebrity gossip, spoiled athletes, and overpaid entertainers to vent.

Somewhat true – on the gossip/athlete/entertainer part. That does take place on Twitter. But you know what? You do NOT have to follow any of them or see any of it. I don't follow a single celebrity or professional athlete who causes a stir on Twitter.

Who do I follow and who follows me? Millionaires. Successful entrepreneurs. Exceptional coaches, mentors, peers, and thought leaders. People who I would have never met without Twitter. People who have helped me and those who I have helped, all without expecting any reciprocation.

Twitter is jam packed with entrepreneurs and great businesspeople, and all you have to do is follow them to learn from what they do and how they connect with people. That is why I love it. But more on that later...

APPLICATION:

1. What myths or objections do you have about social media? It's okay, we all have them. Make a list of them.
2. Now, make a decision to throw them out as you read this book. Have an open mind as we take this journey. Your mind and parachutes have one thing in common: they work better when they're open.
3. Social media will NEVER take the place of face-to-face connecting, but it can greatly contribute to the process. Take a moment to visualize yourself meeting great people through social networking as you create your **Stop Pitching, Start Connecting** strategy.

CHAPTER 3: THE CURRENT STATE OF NETWORK MARKETING AND SOCIAL MEDIA

We've discussed why social media is valuable to your business and debunked the major social networking myths. Before we move onto strategies for your success in social networking, it's important to wrap our mind around the current state.

Here are the five social media personalities I've seen. Keep in mind that as I describe these types of social media users, I mean no offense. As we learn social media, we all make mistakes, just like any newly learned skill.

1. **The people who get it**

These are the people who use social media effectively. It generates traffic to their websites and blogs. Their blogs build their credibility as a thought leader. They join the conversation and maximize exposure and networking opportunities. They have a business page on Facebook with great content and value. They organize their time well and are seen as an expert or looked up to by their peers when it comes to social media.

Most of you reading this book are not in this category yet. Hence why you're reading this book. Kudos for continuing your education and being open to the next great frontier of networking. If you follow the advice, tips, and strategies in this book, and take a long-term, consistent approach to social media, you will reach greener pastures.

There are those of you reading this that are in this category. You get it. You value education and want to learn even more. I hope you can learn a few new tips and ideas to continue perfecting your social media and digital marketing strategy.

2. Those who are lost

They are the aimless, the huddled masses of confused networkers trying to use social media. They don't have a goal. They don't have a purpose. They're inconsistent.

Sometimes they post too often, sometimes too little. They will post every single picture from their vacation on Facebook, but go months without spreading the good news about the benefits of the products or company they represent. They start a Pinterest account, then go months without pinning. They get active on Twitter for three weeks and disappear. They start a blog, get excited and tell people about it, then abandon it before it ever gets traction, drives traffic, or creates leverage.

Another version of the lost is those who can't draw the line. Occasionally (or often), their posts stray to obscene, offensive, divisive, or posting while angry or intoxicated.

3. Those who are selling, selling, selling

"It's called social media for a reason, it's not called marketing media. When people say 'buy this, buy this, buy this,' it doesn't work. You need to build brand equity and social equity, where people like you and trust you," says business owner BK Boreyko.

It's possibly the worst of our breed on social media. Their answer to everything is to "join my team" or "start earning bonuses". They post more than 50% of the time about their opportunity, their company, or their products, in a way that makes people shudder. If social media was a cocktail party or family reunion, you'd avoid them like the plague.

"The biggest mistake I see is the hard sell. Buy, buy, buy, isn't going to work! People want to learn something, be entertained or feel like they matter. If your customers feel like they're being sold something all the time, where is the connection? You should represent something more than what you sell!" branding expert Luke Dancy says.

Humans have developed a sixth sense when it comes to being sold or pitched. They know when someone has an agenda, and all they care about is getting you to whip out your credit card. You see these people and you want to run far away.

Psychologically, our brains see these messages in the same category as someone who constantly spouts negativity, non-stop political ramblings, or in-your-face, holier than thou religious musings.

It's the theme of this book: STOP PITCHING & START CONNECTING. What is it about normal, sane people who join network marketing and all of the sudden turn into the creepy Federated Products couple from the movie *Go*? (Watch the network marketing scene).

We can become the very type of people we despise if we're not careful. Old school network marketing used to be about ambushing people at Denny's and tricking them into coming to your opportunity meeting. It doesn't have to be, wait…, it SHOULDN'T be like that anymore.

Non-stop pitching and selling on social media will not work, and if it does produce minor results, they won't last. We are in the connection economy. Permission marketing is what people are seeking. Trust is sacred and necessary. You CAN use social media effectively as a network marketer without sacrificing your dignity.

If you've fallen into the trap of selling or pitching too often, you've come to the right place. If that's not you, good. You're on the right track already.

4. Time wasters

These social media users are not exclusive to network marketing, but many networkers fall into this mode. They get lost for hours on social media. They get validation from the likes and comments on Facebook. They share links, surveys, cat videos, and odd news stories constantly. Many times they will blindly like every post they see and spend hours on games that don't advance their finances.

Yet, by posting once a day about their company or opportunity, they feel like they've prospected for the day and go right back to spamming the heck out of their online community. It's a sad cycle, but it can be broken.

5. The non-existent

The last type of social media personality is the person who isn't on it. They either believe it's not worthwhile or they're intimidated by it. If they don't see the value, they may be from a generation that grew up without technology or they might have excelled at another type of networking.

Look at all the companies who have refused to adapt to new technologies. Borders Books. Blockbuster Video. Kodak. Slow adopters to new technology or e-commerce had to play major catch up, and many of them never did. Newspapers were almost made extinct by the Internet. Amazon crushed their old school competitors. Failure to innovate and evolve will cost you.

People who aren't using social media at all may carry with them a great deal of wisdom when it comes to connecting. They just need help adapting and learning to use their great skills in a new way.

If you're reading this because you feel like social media is more chore than fun, or more hassle than what it's worth, but you realize you have to do something because social networking is the way of the future, congratulations. It's not easy to drop the ego and admit that you need something, even when you don't fully understand why.

If you fall into the group of people who are intimidated by social media, I will strip it down to its birthday suit so you can see it's harmless and can be tackled by anyone.

Do me a huge favor while you read this book and put into practice the principles and application: don't compare yourself to others. You are unique. No one can be you and you cannot be them. There is room for all of us to be great with social media.

Don't measure your success by how many likes, followers, fans, friends, retweets, endorsements, or favorites people get. Comparing is a recipe for unhappiness and being unfulfilled. Be yourself, and you'll get where you want to go.

APPLICATION:

1. Which social media personality are you? Which do you want to be? Congratulate yourself for reading this book and taking action. Make the commitment to follow the application and advice so you can be social media savvy.
2. Take a few minutes to scan the posts on one of your social media feeds. What type of posts do you find engaging? What annoys you? What posts are receiving a lot of engagement, comments, likes, retweets, etc.?
3. For the next few days, gauge how much time you are spending on social media, watching television, and other activities. Where can you carve out uninterrupted time to work on your strategy?

SECTION 2: STAKE YOUR CLAIM IN SOCIAL MEDIA

Like most of us, I wasn't on Twitter or Facebook right away. While I like to be an early adapter (I owned an mp3 player LONG before anyone had heard of an iPod), I also like to do things long term. I don't want to jump on something if it's not necessarily going to stick around. I like to watch and learn, then once I decide I'm all in, there's no going back.

My social media light bulb lit up, ironically, when I started spending more and more time on the road, meeting with people face to face. I realized that I like to meet people and network, but it's not as easy when you're not face to face.

By traveling and networking around the world, I started to appreciate that there were like-minded people all over who were looking to connect with people like me. Yet, when I wasn't on the road, I didn't get that exposure. Enter **social media**.

My friend Steve Gutzler told me he started building his Twitter followers and network locally in the Seattle area, then branched out from there. I experienced the same result. I found that there were like-minded people in San Diego who I would never have met without social media.

Isn't that incredible? There are people in your hometown, looking for connections like you, who you would never get introduced to otherwise. That was a game-changer for me.

Up until then, I had been a reluctant social media user. That's putting it lightly (you'll read my Twitter story in an upcoming chapter). I guess you could say I was very reluctant, and was on the fence whether I thought social networks were complete time wasters. Have you ever felt that way?

Once I found out there were like-minded people out there and I wouldn't get to meet them unless I was on social media, the light bulb went off like a strobe. **Social media was going to be what I made it.**

I've now met multiple people through Twitter who live in San Diego. I've met them face to face, hiked with them, talked business with them, referred them to others, and even interviewed them as part of this book. As Steve suggested, I started local and now have met people across the globe.

I consider social networking sites to be the future of networking, or at least how to glue your connections together once you've networked. Now when I meet people on a plane, in an airport, at an event, or anywhere I go, I always ask if they are on Twitter, Facebook, LinkedIn, or another social network where I can continue my connection with them.

With social media, I feel like I've got an all access pass to great thought leaders, business experts, and people in my niche. People who I would have never met or been able to contact five years ago are now readily available to me.

You've probably already experienced the benefits of being able to keep in contact with family members, friends, and associates through Facebook. Maybe you've snagged a great recipe off of Pinterest or been recommended or endorsed on LinkedIn. Possibly you have watched a how-to video on YouTube or you were inspired by someone's blog.

The benefits of social media are seemingly endless. Deeper connections. Trust. Recommendations and referrals. But maybe you've dipped your toes in the cool waters of social networking without really understanding how to leverage it. It's time to start thinking about who you want to be in social networking and what you want your personal brand look like.

As you read this section keep your BIG WHY in mind. Why do you do what you do? What is your dream? How does your big why affect the choices you will make as you determine how you interact with social media?

CHAPTER 4: LET'S TAKE A STEP BACK

Good news. It's time to stop a moment for a breath and some realization.

You are involved in a real business in a super-successful industry that brings in over $160 billion a year and pays back roughly 40% of it to their customers. What other industry does that? None that I know of. What other industry taps into the most powerful, genuine advertising in the world – word-of-mouth advertising – and gives you an opportunity to grow a business based on your personal brand and the trust you build? Very few.

You are on the forefront of a great movement, and you are learning to use social media as a vehicle to open up your warm market like never before. You're going to do it by being 100% YOU. You're going to lay aside the stress and enjoy connecting through social media, finding like-minded people who will surely become your friends, and who just might also become a business partner, client, or customer. You're going to keep it real by CARING about people and setting aside the temptation to feel needy. You have permission to enjoy people for who they are as you connect through social media.

When you genuinely care about the people you're connecting with, you'll resist the urge to sell on social media. When you have a marathon mentality you won't pitch them whenever they show the slightest interest in what you do. Let's build relationships and trust so people will organically ask you, "What are you up to?"

Now think about the easiest way to learn. Isn't it by watching someone else who is really good at what they do? Or better yet, working alongside them? The Internet is full of people you can study and learn from. As you watch someone farther down the road than you are, and as you read and apply the strategies in this book, there are a few things to keep in mind:

Share what you've learned. People put out content, training, and inspiration to impact people in a positive way. What good would that impact be if it wasn't used AND shared with others? Take what you like from this book, from the advice within, make it your own, and help others.

Think of yourself as a disciple. Take what you learn and teach it to someone else. No matter what your religious or spiritual beliefs are, look at the way Jesus led people and taught people. He was only one man, one leader. He knew there was no way he could reach every person he needed to. So, what did he do? He found 12 people to teach his message to and expected them to take it further. He didn't try to get to everyone. JB Glossinger relayed this principal perfectly. "I think the problem is people to spread themselves too thin, trying to meet too many people, and that's what slows them down," he said. JB is an entrepreneur and podcaster who runs MorningCoach.com, helping thousands of subscribers with his daily 'CoachCasts'.

Develop your own way of doing things. Don't try to be a carbon-copy of your favorite social media success story. Learn from this book, but constantly look for ways you can take the strategies and make them unique to YOU. I'm going to give you step by step directions in some cases, but most of the approaches in this book should be taken as guidelines, not gospel. No two snowflakes are identical, and the same goes for building your personal brand through social media and network marketing.

Stay encouraged as you begin this important learning curve! You now have a competitive advantage over all other networkers who aren't using social media effectively, or at all. Use it wisely. Anyone can get trained on social media, just like anyone can write a book if they really want to. But few do. Every entrepreneur and networker on the planet can read this book, yet less than 5% will actually put the principles into action. Think about a time when you heard a motivational speaker who sparked an idea in you. You were inspired and excited. Did you take action on this new found motivation? If you did, you were in the top 1%. Most people won't do it. By taking action on what you learn from this book, you will be gaining a competitive advantage in your niche.

APPLICATION:

1. Think about the Big Why, the reason you are building a business. How does that legitimize your process with social media?
2. Make a list of people you can follow up with on social media without pitching them on anything Now, go connect. Contact them and just say hello. Comment on their posts. Do this with 3-5 people a day.
3. What approach have you seen on social media that you love? What expert do you enjoy following? Why? How can you implement what you've learned and still be 100% YOU?

CHAPTER 5: YOUR PERSONAL BRAND

"You've got to be able to scream from the top of a mountain what you do. You've got to believe in yourself." – JB Glossinger

Now the fun begins: the journey of discovery of yourself and your brand. Your personal brand – who you are, what you stand for, what you know, how you carry yourself, etc. – is a BIG part of people deciding to be in business with you. It can be the biggest differentiator between you, your company, and another opportunity or no opportunity at all.

Personal branding makes **you** the main brand of your business. In network marketing, people are choosing to do business with you. Sure, you represent a product or line of products which are made available through a company. That company pays you, provides tools, a website, back office, etc. But I can buy from anyone at that company. Most companies have at least a few hundred distributors, if not thousands. Why would I buy from you?

You are the best brand you've got. Not your products, not your compensation plan, not the company you represent, etc. Sure, those all play a role. But people join and buy because of you. Your **personal brand** is critical to your success.

Bruce Van Horn is a speaker, author, and life coach with almost 300,000 followers on Twitter. He says, "Your brand is everything. Your brand is your reputation. Your brand is your story. Without a story, a brand means nothing. Creating things like a podcast, a YouTube channel, and a social media presence gives you an outlet to tell your story."

Bruce continues, "I can find a dozen people doing what you do and selling what you sell. In network marketing, people want to be associated with you more than the company you represent."

Why it's important - people are watching

People can find more details about you than ever before thanks to the Internet and social media. For the most part, you get to choose what they see! However, on the flipside, if you choose to avoid developing a personal brand online, prospects and potential business partners will seek it out anyway.

"Perspective people who could work with you are checking out your Facebook page and seeing what you have out there on social media," states Chris Freytag. People are looking at your social media accounts. You need to create a personal brand that sells you.

You can edify and articulate your body of work

My good friend, speaker, author, and innovation expert Stephen Shapiro gave me terrific advice: if you want to leverage who you are and what you know so people look at you as an expert, you must articulate your body of work.

Social media gives you an unprecedented, nearly 100% free opportunity to articulate what you know. You can establish an online presence that edifies what you've accomplished, what you know, and your experience. When new people find you through social networking, you will already have credibility with them because they can see your work expressed, or visible in front of them.

You can have a rebirth

Many times in our personal or professional lives, our associations get stale. They are no longer pushing us forward and keeping us sharp. They may even be holding us back.

The crowd you hang out with, both in person and online, can typecast you as one type of person. They think they know your experience, past, weaknesses, and strengths. It can be very hard to have familiar people see you in a new, elevated way.

Let's say you've had the same job for 10 years. You have the same routines. Soccer on Saturday with the kids. A couple vacations a year.

Now you start your own home-based business. You're involved in personal development. You're growing as a leader and a business person. You're an entrepreneur.

A big part of that battle is mental. You need to think of yourself as an entrepreneur and successful business person. Visualizing yourself every day as a self-employed mover and shaker is a daily ritual you must perform. This can be difficult when the people who know you could never picture you this way. They see you as one particular person and thinking of you as a successful business owner is tough for them, if not impossible.

In building a great business, you may find you need a rebirth so you can meet new people who see you in a different light. It's not about completely divorcing old relationships (although there probably ARE some you want to do that with), it's about meeting people who see what you're up to and want to help you get there.

Social media is a great opportunity for any rebirth you need, especially starting a new social media channel. Twitter and Pinterest come to mind as sites that most networkers are not using or aren't using effectively. By joining these sites, you can have a rebirth, meet new people, and start associating with like-minded professionals.

This doesn't necessarily mean they will buy from you or join your organization. And if you constantly pitch people for this, you're missing the point of social media and this book. And if you're asking yourself, "If they're not part of my organization, then how could they help me?", then I'm going to ask you to open your mind and broaden your thoughts.

A quick example….

A lot of my friends, former co-workers, and family on Facebook have known me for decades or longer. They knew me before I could speak from stage, moderate a conference call or meeting, or emcee an event. They know me as genuine and a person who creates solutions, but also somewhat shy and reserved.

It would be very, very hard for some of these associates to think of me as an author, speaker, consultant, coach, or people person. Maybe even impossible. If they think that way, there's simply no way they could help propel me forward or lift me up. They may even subconsciously work against me, as they potentially meet great people to refer me to, but never would because they don't think of me in that light.

I joined Twitter and listed myself as a speaker, author, and coach. By employing a strategy of tweeting and connecting that worked, I was able to meet other coaches, speakers, entrepreneurs, etc. These new contacts right away thought of me as one of them. And because I was adding value to their lives through connecting, content, and promoting them, they are likely to do the same for me. This has already happened many times over.

I hope you're starting to get the picture. As a networker, if you want to live the life of your dreams and make an incredible income as a self-made businessperson, your associations matter. They will either hold you back or help you get where you want to go. You always need to be evaluating your relationships and forging new ones. And how can you find a new group of people who will instantly see you as the person you see yourself as? Social media.

If you could use a rebirth of sorts, you've come to the right place.

Become a thought leader

Along the lines of a rebirth, you can utilize social media not only to connect with thought leaders, but become one. This is a big deal.

The more you are thought of as a leader, the more people will be drawn to you. The more people who are drawn to you, the more selective you can be on who you work with and who you grow your business with. That's right, you can be selective if you're willing to put in the work.

This is where I see a lot of networkers, both young and old, and at varying success levels, shun social media because there isn't the instant gratification or overnight millions. They want a lead generation system or online leads to drop like water out of a faucet.

Most people who create a successful lead generation system are NOT willing to share how they did it. Plus, most of us don't have the financial resources, risk tolerance, patience, or technical know-how to make this happen.

However, if you're willing to be consistent and have a long-term approach to your social media and online platform, you could create something that few people have and even fewer are willing to go after – an endless source of interested people flowing into your prospecting pipeline.

By employing social media to establish yourself as a thought leader, people will come to YOU seeking business advice, coaching, guidance, AND partnership. And that's when network marketing gets really fun – when you no longer have to pitch people or continually present and instead have people beating down your door to work with you. It can happen. Repeat after me – it can happen. I've seen it over and over.

The most lucrative businesses have a leader with vision and charisma. With the popularity of social media, it's never been easier to establish your platform as a charismatic thought leader to attract people like a magnet.

Social media has made it easier than ever to develop your personal brand

Jamie Stewart's statement on why network marketers need to embrace social media to build their personal brand, "People spend as much time on social media as they do on TV. In fact they are often on both at same time. The television industry is seeing this and using it to engage with hashtags and questions during shows. Direct selling has always been about social proof - people recommending products. So social media is perfect for this. It's still a person-to-person business and social media allows you do this like never before."

Twitter, Facebook, LinkedIn, Pinterest, blogging, videos, websites, tweetchats, podcasts – the list is almost endless. All of these tools at your disposal make it easier than ever in history to create your personal brand.

Before social media and before blogs, and before YouTube, Amazon, and iTunes, if you had a great message on personal development, how could you get that message out to people?

You could write a book. But how would you market it? How would people hear about it?

You could hold conference calls. But again, how would people know they were there? Where could they get a schedule?

You could create a networking meeting group, but once again, how the heck would people hear about it?

Before it was so easy to create a platform online, you didn't have many choices. Essentially, all you could do was buy advertising, unless you knew someone who would throw you a bone and give you a free mention in a newspaper, magazine, or at an event. You could also try a snail mail campaign or rely on face-to-face networking.

Very few of us could afford to buy advertising month after month, especially if a few trials didn't work. Think about how many billboards, radio spots, television ads, and other gimmicks McDonald's has to use to try to maintain your attention.

If you have any experience in network marketing in the 1990's, you probably knew a networker or small group of networkers who were successful because they found a winning formula for placing classified or magazine ads or doing radio spots. However, that almost never became mainstream and almost always fizzled out after a period of time. Yet it seemed hundreds of people would look at these successful advertisers as the flavor of the day and try to learn from and emulate them with very little success.

Fast forward. Now you CAN get the word out. Now you CAN develop a platform and network of people who help you spread the word.

Think about it. If I plan a conference call for next week where I want to train people how to think like an entrepreneur and share ideas of how to make income outside of a regular job, I can be spreading the word instantly. No longer do I need to wait until the classifieds come out Wednesday or Sunday. I simply plan a call, email it to my network, and encourage them to share it on social media. I can post it on my Facebook page, promote it for a few dollars so it reaches dramatically more people, tweet it, pin it, create a 60 second video, etc.

Within an hour I can have thousands of people exposed to it and already signing up for my call. And by exchanging their email address for the login details, I'm creating a database of contacts and prospects for the future.

Mitzi Dulan is known as America's Nutrition Expert. She's also been the nutritionist for several professional sports teams, including most recently serving in that capacity for the 2014 American League Champion Kansas City Royals. I believe she summed up personal branding through social media perfectly when she told me, "The wonderful thing about social media is that people who would never have developed a large following from lack of a marketing budget can now have a voice and **build a platform."**

Leverage

Leverage is one of the most powerful concepts in business. My definition of leverage is to maximize your contacts, experience, expertise, and knowledge for mutual benefit. It's gaining every advantage possible, but in a very authentic way, a way that supports and promotes other people too.

Many network marketers I've known look at every person and think, how can I get them to join my business? How can I approach them? What can I say to get them to meet with me?

This is a linear, short-sighted approach. Great networkers, no matter what business they're in, see opportunities everywhere to leverage relationships, networks, meetings, and connections. This leverage I speak of is genuine. It's not using someone, but leveraging their skills and contacts and vice versa.

You know not every person will join your team. It's imperative to find the right people and make the most out of your relationships.

If you choose to try and pitch everyone relentlessly, you will have many, many frustrating days and most likely never hit your potential. However, if you make the most out of your connections and try to connect with as many people as possible, your marketing and prospecting funnel will always be filled. You can be *selective* about who you work with.

By having a broader mindset focused on **leverage**, it becomes a two-way street. Not only can you leverage relationships, but they can leverage you. This win-win strategy will greatly increase what Steve Gutzler calls "referability." Isn't that what we're all looking for?

"You have to be careful of selling and self-promoting, you don't have to be afraid to do it, but doing it sparingly. I use strategies to draw people close to me and gain trust in me. I want them to recommend me. We're all looking for **referability.** People know my motive is healthy and balanced. I want an authentic nature that draws people towards me," says Gutzler, who is a big-time influencer on social media.

If this isn't the right time for someone to buy or join, the next best thing is that they become a person who refers people to you. If you can get someone thinking like you, trusting you, and liking what you do, they will recommend you whenever possible. However, if you focus mainly on pitching, you will be avoided, not recommended.

For example, you don't need tires very often. Every few years or more you need to replace your tires. So, if the local tire shop was sending you sales material, emailing you, calling you, and you still had a good 25,000 miles left on your tires, you would become desensitized or worse, annoyed by their constant marketing to you.

However, if they kept in touch with you, gave you free tire rotations every 5,000 miles, and gave you great service no matter what you purchased, you will have good feelings about them. The benefits of doing business with them are evident, even if you're not currently in the market.

Because you have these good feelings about them, the next time you hear a friend, family member, or associate say they need tires, who are you going to recommend? The pushy, upselling tire shop that markets to you relentlessly, or the friendly tire shop who cares about you no matter how much, if any, money you spend?

Do you see how connecting and leveraging relationships can help you when you least expect it? It's a lot more fun than constantly pitching and pushing on people, driving them away and/or having them ignore you. It works, and in our **connection economy** you can capitalize on it. Leverage it, my friends.

"When people are recognized and acknowledged they want to associate with you. They want to do more with you. I don't have to tell them what I do for a living. I show up and acknowledge them and that makes all the difference." –Lolly Daskal, coach, speaker, author, and Founder of Lead From Within, a global consultancy firm. Lolly was also named one of the Top Thought Leaders to Follow by *The Huffington Post.*

Finding that "perfect for you" customer or business partner

Fitness personality Chris Freytag loves personal branding through social media because it allows you to find what she calls that "perfect for you client."

She says, "Social media allows me to connect directly with consumers and fans and the like-minded person, the person who likes me, my **perfect for you client.** Before social media it was hard. I use to do blanket marketing, flyers to zip codes, throw things against the wall to see what stuck. I wasn't able to contact my perfect for me clients."

Freytag continues, "With social media, I've already crossed that hump. I'm already marketing to them. No more blind marketing. I'm connecting with the people who want to connect with me. Why waste dollars on people who don't care about you? You don't need 10,000 eyes or followers, you need 100-200 good ones."

I love that she feels like she's no longer paying for advertising or marketing to people who aren't looking for what she's got to offer. The same applies to your business. I've worked with literally thousands of well-meaning people who spend dollars and time trying to reach people who are NOT interested in what they have to offer.

Remember our 97%? Well, there's the 30% who may never be interested or who aren't good candidates for your business. I've seen so many good people get their dreams crushed by working with the wrong people.

With social media, you can find that "perfect for you" prospect or business partner. They're waiting for you.

APPLICATION:

1. How do you want to be known or perceived? What is your personal brand? Write down a list of attributes and strengths you have. Include your experience and expertise.
2. Now think about yourself as a leader – attracting and working with the right people. Visualize it. How are people seeing you as a leader? What would they say about your strengths? Write these down like they're already happening.
3. Spend a few minutes each day visualizing yourself as a thought leader on social media, finding those "perfect for you" people and growing your "referability." Get your subconscious mind working for you by pointing it in the right direction.

SECTION 3: BUILDING YOUR SOCIAL MEDIA FOUNDATION

"I just can't make sense of it all. I don't even know where to begin," said Tara.

Tara felt overwhelmed by all the choices in social media. She felt like she needed to do them all, so that's what she tried. She spent a month starting a Pinterest account. Started three different blogs. Gave up on Twitter after two weeks. Found Instagram confusing among all her other platforms. Didn't know what her message was or would be. You get the picture.

Once I started working with her, we broke it down to simple building blocks. When asked what was the one thing, just one thing she wanted to do online if she could do nothing else, she wanted a website. So I coached her to start there. In the process of creating a website, she found her voice.

Forgetting all other online channels, Tara focused on simple content for her website, specifically her 'about' page. She reviewed other 'about' pages and became educated on what she liked and didn't like. Once she took that first step, the light bulb went off. Suddenly, she knew exactly how she wanted to impact the world. She tapped into her passion and message. From there, her social media choices seemed to just fall into place.

As we get into building your foundation, relax and enjoy the ride. We'll break it down into bite-sized chunks so you can start to take action and feel good about it.

CHAPTER 6: TIME TO GET EDUCATED

Most well-seasoned social media users will tell you it's easy to get overwhelmed by all the choices you have when it comes to picking a social media site. I've personally worked with hundreds of networkers who have let the phrases, "I don't get it," "I'll never understand it," or "It's too overwhelming," get the best of them. They think that there's some secret formula to overnight success with social networking.

Like a jigsaw puzzle, if you line up the pieces correctly, you'll find what works for you. But it will take time and a determination to learn before you discover the path that is uniquely YOU.

Anyone who tells you that you can build a social media following that trusts you, likes you, and wants to buy from you in a matter of weeks or short months is not giving the full truth. They may be trying to make money off of you, inexperienced, or misinformed.

You may feel inferior, confused, or lost right now because of your lack of social media savvy. That's okay! Feel that way for a minute and then let's get busy.

One sure fire way to get past ignorance or confusion is **education**. With the internet today, there is no excuse why you can't get a nearly free education in social media. Instead of falling for some scam to teach you how to use Facebook or blog for money, you'll have enough knowledge to be dangerous. Not only dangerous, but enough smarts to pick and choose the RIGHT programs to actually pay for.

Yes, there are programs, classes, mastermind groups, etc., that are worth your money. But unless you invest time and sweat equity in your education, you're going to think you can pay someone to make you a social media expert overnight.

"Social media is not a magic bullet. Without a strategic and creative approach you won't succeed," according to Geoff Talbot, founder of Seven Sentences and a consultant on brand, marketing, and voice development.

News flash: **THERE IS NO MAGIC BULLET!**

It's like that famous Thomas Edison quote – the social media magic bullet is "disguised in boots and overalls because it looks like work." Because it is work! Building a business, creating an online following, keeping a marriage together, it doesn't matter – anything worthwhile takes effort and dedication. If it were easy, everyone would be doing it.

You're different. Acknowledge it. Say it out loud. You're going to set yourself apart by working for it. You may not have the most experience or financial resources, but you've got plenty of 'get after it' in your blood. And that's what it takes.

Part of this is working smart, not just hard. Let's start by getting educated. It's simple, but you have to be willing to take the time and effort to do it. Are you willing to do the little things that most people won't do? Are you going to complain and whine about being overwhelmed or are you going to do something about it?

Good. You got this book because you're ready to learn. You're ready to get past that fog of confusion, get clear, and start taking action.

Let's start by asking yourself a few questions. *You* asking yourself questions. You do it all the time, so now let's track those questions.

Whenever you have a question about social media or personal branding, write it down. Write it on a notes page on your phone or computer. Put it in a notebook or journal. Keep track of your questions so you can get answers.

For a long, long time I wanted to blog. I read blogs, but I let ignorance get the best of me. Lack of understanding the technology side of blogging – setting up a website and hosting and the design – held me back for years.

I felt like the out of shape, unfit person walking into a gym for the first time. Intimidated. Nervous. Ignorant. Uneducated. That hot, embarrassed feeling crept over me.

Education on blogging is readily available. Both paid and free. But I let intimidation and the unknown overwhelm me. My feet were in concrete, put there by my head. Then I got educated.

I met bloggers on Twitter. I asked them questions like: What's the best way to get started? What web hosting do you use? Do you use WordPress or something else? What training do you recommend?

There's magic in the words – *can you help me?* Many successful people love to mentor and help others achieve their goals.

I look back on and I'm a little disappointed and embarrassed it took me years of wanting to blog before finally getting started. It took determination and education to get me going.

Don't make my blogging mistake. Take matters into your own hands and get educated, starting right now. You are in control of your education. Take the reins today and take advantage of all the information available to you.

Following is free

One of the simplest things you can do to learn social media is follow people who are doing it well. Because social media posts are readily available, you can view almost anyone's strategy and learn from it.

Following someone is free education. All it takes is a few minutes a day to review what they've posted, and how they interact with current and potential customers, fans, and peers.

Here's how you can get a free course on social media from your favorite experts out there:

Twitter: You can follow anybody on Twitter, so pick a handful of people in your niche or that you admire, and follow them today. Take a few minutes a day to see how, what, and when they're posting. You can also follow a few companies to see how they interact with fans and customers.

This is the primary method I used to learn Twitter. I followed many of the people who contributed to this book. I observed what they did. I asked them questions and interacted with them. I shared their content. I saw how many people were sharing their content. I watched them connect with people.

Facebook: With Facebook you will want to 'like' a few pages from companies, musical artists, or business people. Many of them use Facebook as one of their primary methods to keep their fans and customers updated and release new information. They will drive traffic to their Facebook pages and website by holding contests and posting relevant, interesting information to engage people.

Education doesn't need to take hours. By spending five minutes on Facebook simply observing what people are posting, what you like, what you don't like, and what is working for the people you're watching, you can start to get a feel for your strategy. Never be afraid to jump in and simply ask people questions too!

Pinterest: Google the top 100 Pinterest users and follow a few of them. See how they pin and repin. Observe the type of things that are pinned to boards.

Instagram: what types of images are being shared? Follow people you know or businesses you like. Pay attention to hashtag use and frequency of pictures.

Blogs: Whether it's a written blog, YouTube video, or audio podcast, blogs are another fantastically free resource to expand your social media education. Subscribe to a couple blogs, YouTube channels, and podcasts. Spend time each week absorbing this material. If you don't like it, unsubscribe. If you like it, comment and share on your social media.

Time management is critical when it comes to your education. You can be sitting in the same place a year from now wishing you had learned more, or you can take action. With self-paced education, it's on you to make time for it. It doesn't need to take hours. But it will take focused time.

Is it important to you? Are you willing to put in the work? Then schedule the time to get your education. STOP telling yourself you can't learn this, don't have time, you don't get it, it's stupid, or there's some magic bullet to help you understand it overnight. You can do this. Let's put in the effort and let the knowledge compound over time. Then you'll look back and say, "I can't believe how much I've learned!"

Training is out there – you have to want it

There are enough free webinars, teleclasses, video trainings, books, how-to websites, and training courses for you to learn everything you need to know about using social media effectively as a businessperson.

Mashable.com is a great place to start. They have a lot of tutorials for social media. Most social networking sites have their own extensive help sections that are very useful too. Sometimes the best assistance is the most obvious.

A few things to keep in mind with all of this information readily available to you:

Remember the theme of the book – **STOP pitching and START connecting**. You can learn every insider tip you want, but if you sell instead of building relationships and trust, you're going to struggle.

To avoid becoming overwhelmed, use trusted sources. Social media theories are everywhere and unfortunately some can actually do harm to your personal brand. Before you tap into just anyone's training methods, talk to people who have used them. Research their website and Facebook page. Review their tweets and posts.

Good salespeople can draw you in with their marketing, so make yourself an informed consumer. Even with 'free' training, it still costs you time. If you implement the wrong strategy, it can cost you thousands of dollars in the long run.

If you like one particular person's coaching or a specific website's training, use them again. Revisit training that worked. Get more instruction from your trusted source. If they don't offer a topic you're looking for, ask them for a recommendation.

On a recent trip to San Francisco, I wanted to take a private tour of the city and customize the visit for my family's first time to the Bay Area. I spent time researching tour companies and settled on one with fantastic reviews. However, when I called them to book the excursion, they were sold out for that date.

My next question – who else do you recommend? Because I had done my research, I already had a level of trust of this tour company, so their recommendation carried weight with me. The owner referred me to another great tour guide. Our visit was perfect, thanks in large part to me doing my research and an awesome recommendation.

When it comes to your ongoing social media education, do your research and when you find a trusted source, seek recommendations.

I've worked with many networkers who got sold into one person's system of duplication training after doing zero research. They spent all kinds of money and time on their courses, only to be no better off in the end. Worse, they found out that hundreds of other people were getting this so-called one-on-one mentoring with lackluster results.

Do your due diligence my friends. Just because you consider yourself a novice or even an intermediate, it doesn't mean you need to be naïve or ignorant.

Lastly, your social networking education really comes down to common sense. If something seems too good to be true, it probably is. If the trainer is asking you to spent $997 on their proven system, research them. Talk to their clients. Talk to them. If they won't respond to your messages, you probably don't want to work with them. If they don't include a money-back guarantee, don't give them your hard-earned cash.

"Don't sign up to an online program that promises you success but does not spend a significant portion of time helping you to find your voice," advises Geoff Talbot.

Let me Google that for you

I get asked a lot of questions about social media and personal branding. A LOT of questions. Some of them are deep and require me to get to know someone before coaching them. Other times, people are just looking for quick answers. And sometimes people just want to be told what to do.

To be great at social media and use it to help build your personal brand and income, you've got to be resourceful. Fortunately, one of the greatest resources the world has ever seen is readily at your disposal, and it's FREE!

It's called Google. I know you've heard of it. I know you've probably used it.

Here's the thing – if you can get your answer in 30 seconds through a Google search, you do NOT need training on it!

I'm mostly talking about technical details and quick tips. Technology can feel intimidating, but it doesn't have to be. Obviously this isn't a technical book. And why? Because all of that training is available with just a few clicks and a few minutes. This book is about your social media **strategy**.

For quick, technical details, don't throw up your arms and give up. Google will take you to instructions and videos that will show you step-by-step how to overcome almost any technical challenge you have.

I get asked simple questions all the time like, "How do I use Twitter?" When really the question should be, "How can I maximize Twitter to explode my contacts and help my business?"

This book will help you with the real meat of using social networking the right way as a networker, with methods that will add connections and resources for the long haul. I want to help you develop a strategy that works for you. I want you to establish your own personal brand so your income and influence become limitless.

So Google the easy questions. Don't make someone just give you the answers. You'll be better off being resourceful and learning it on your own.

Mindset

Before we dip into your strategy and get rolling on growing your social media presence, let's talk about mindset more specifically.

So much of education is having the **desire** to learn. Do you just want answers and someone to tell you what to do, or do you want to learn?

When you get educated, you can then educate others. You're part of the experience. You can mentor and teach your organization. That's leadership.

Right now, commit to the mindset that you are a leader, and as a leader you're hungry to learn social media. You've got to want it!

Chances are you learned to drive a car. When you learned to drive, you were excited and hungry. You were determined to learn because the result of this knowledge was freedom. You were probably instructed by a parent and/or a driving class. But the real reason you learned was experience. You did it. You got behind the wheel. You hit the brakes too hard. You tried to start a stick shift without the clutch in. It was the hands-on experience that really gave you an education in driving.

Social media is very similar. Everything I'm teaching and sharing with you is geared to get you behind the wheel. I can't give you all the answers. I hope you don't want all the answers. If it were that easy, everyone would tap into the power of social media to drive their business forward.

I learned social media through experience. The people I interviewed for this book learned through experience. Every person I interviewed for this book and every associate I've worked with started somewhere. Yes, they may have got help or worked with great mentors. That's what you're doing right now (kudos, by the way). But ultimately they started the car, made mistakes and tried things. Some things worked, others did not. They created their own personal brand and crafted a strategy that worked for them.

Your mindset is critical right now. Of course it's critical to your success as an entrepreneur and business owner, but just as crucial when it comes to learning new things.

No matter where you're at in your networking career and social media knowledge, you need the right mindset to get where you want to go. You've got to be hungry.

For almost 10 years I coached youth sports – football, basketball, and baseball. Who were my favorite kids to work with? The kids who were hungry. Hungry to learn. Hungry to improve. Hungry to have fun and win. Are you hungry to win with social media?

Ready to build your social media strategy to get results? Good. Stay hungry my friends.

APPLICATION:

1. Start a questions log or notebook. Every time you have a question about social media, especially technical details (i.e. how do I connect my Instagram and Facebook accounts?), write it down so you can research it later.
2. Google your questions and experience the answers. Use the help section of the site you're on, it probably has what you're looking for.
3. Visit Mashable.com or Google free training and tips you can start applying right away.

CHAPTER 7: TIPS ON CHOOSING THE RIGHT SOCIAL MEDIA NETWORK(S) FOR YOU

"There's no cookie cutter way to do social media. It has to do authentically with who you are and what you want to accomplish. Let's figure out what's good for you." –Lolly Daskal

With so many social media sites/channels to choose from, which is right for you?

There is no perfect answer for everyone to determine which channel(s) to use. Pick a channel or two, but there could be some trial and error involved. In future chapters I'll go through your social media options in detail, but let's get some big picture concepts in place so you can ask intelligent questions and formulate wise approaches to social media as you begin to think more specifically about which channel(s) you want to engage with.

As we move forward, have an open mind. Just because you don't fully understand Twitter or Pinterest yet, doesn't mean you can't understand them and use them to establish your online platform.

As you will read later in the book, my Twitter story is typical. I started it, didn't understand it, hated it, and stopped. I started to make progress when I got a little help and took a different approach. The *connecting* approach. Now it's my favorite social media medium.

Get some help

Let me expand on a point from the section you just read on getting an education. The best place to start in designing your social media approach is to ask questions. Ask people you know and trust how they chose their social media channels. Pay close attention to what my interviewees say in this book too.

Please do NOT ask people who are biased, uneducated, or old fashioned about this topic. When I coached a married couple about using Twitter to grow their warm market, they were very hesitant. I gave them a list of benefits and told them I would work with them to create a winning strategy. I thought highly of them and saw them struggling to expand their connections outside the small town where they lived.

Well, the next day the woman posted on Facebook asking her friends and family what they think of Twitter. The result? Overwhelmingly negative feedback. People didn't get it. They said it was a waste of time. It was only for celebrity gossip. Blah, blah, blah.

Listen, if I wanted to find out what people thought about the Honda Accord, would I ask Toyota Camry owners? If I wanted to know why people like their iPhones, would I ask android users? No and no.

Bottom line was that this couple did NOT have an open mind about social media. They were very old school with their thinking, and then let chickens talk them out of being eagles.

Be smart. You are reading this because you know social media is here to stay and you can capitalize on it. Don't ask the wrong people for advice. The best question falls flat when the wrong person is asked.

Limit your channels – start small

The best social media channels have defined purposes. Twitter, Facebook, blogging, podcasts, LinkedIn, Pinterest, YouTube, etc., are all the same in that they are social networking, but they are all very different when it comes to how people use them, who uses them, and why.

I've worked with many people who open an Instagram account, a Twitter account, expand their Facebook presence to include a business page, start connecting on LinkedIn, and pay someone to set up a blog for them. It makes me overwhelmed just writing about it. **By trying to do too much you'll accomplish nothing.** The old adage about a man who chases two rabbits catches none is absolutely true.

"I was advised early on to drive a stake in one of the social mediums," says Steve Gutzler. "Unless you have a big staff or team, you're not going to spread over six to eight channels."

Start small. You probably already have a Facebook account. Great. Let's start using it consistently and elevating your personal brand. Then, let's pick another site, either Pinterest, Instagram, or Twitter and start using it slowly but consistently.

Next, let's add a blog of some sort – either written, video, or audio and if that's too much, then that's okay, you can hold off for now. Within the next 90 days you need to be more proficient, consistent, and dedicated to your online platform and brand. Take a deep breath; I'm going to help you get there.

Maybe it will help to know this. Unless you're Richard Branson or some big shot, most of us started at zero. Everyone I interviewed for this book started with zero likes, followers, blog subscribers, etc. They were all willing to put in the work to build to a place of success. If they can use social media to help build their business, so can you.

Be determined

Fierce determination is essential. When I jumped into Twitter for the second time (again, story coming up later) I was so determined to understand it that I would not accept my confusion or desire to throw in the towel. I realized there was so much potential that I would do almost anything to make it work for me.

You MUST have dedication and drive to understand how to use social media like a pro. It's going to take time. There will be some failure. There will be times when someone unfollows you or no one reads that blog you felt was genius. There will be days when you feel envious of others.

All of this is normal, but it can cause you to slip away into obscurity for weeks or months, completely undermining what you've started to build. Don't be that person you know who starts and doesn't finish, even if that has been a way you've coped in the past, commit now to be a finisher and take the marathon approach with social media.

It's time to **stop pitching and start connecting** if you want to stand out. And it starts with your determination to do things a little differently.

What type of social media do you enjoy and what works for you?

"People should pick the things they like! New social networks are popping up every week and most are trendy and fade away, or get bought up by Google or Facebook. Unless you are a business looking to market on a large scale, you should target just one or two social platforms that feel right for you," says Luke Dancy.

Lolly Daskal says, "The platforms I use are Twitter, Pinterest, and LinkedIn. Why? They work for me. People have short attention spans, so writing 140 characters works for me. I like to say it as short as possible. I use Twitter to get it out there, then I write articles on LinkedIn. Pinterest is a visual for me. I tap into different ways people like to get information."

These experts know what works for them. They learned it through trial and error, by taking action, and experience. What's interesting about the experts interviewed for this book is that they all made different social media choices that fit their own taste and needs. And they found success. Just know that it may take some time to figure out what's your best fit.

You can make just about any social network work for you, but if you don't enjoy it, or worse, if you HATE it, you're probably not going to do what it takes to use it well and create connections.

It's like the first time you learned anything complicated or even scary. For me, it was making sales calls and following up over the phone many years ago. It seemed like the phone weighed 100 pounds. But once my determination took over, I took action, and tasted some success, I got past my fear and inexperience.

I encourage you to do the same. A new channel will take time, mistakes, effort, consistency, persistence, and desire. You may have tried Pinterest or Twitter in the past and didn't get it. Maybe you gave up too soon. Maybe you need a little more determination.

Make a pact with yourself right now. You're going to follow the strategies in this book to build an online platform, grow your personal brand, and use social media like a champ. No throwing in the towel. No saying "I don't get it." Get out of your head and into the game. Change your perception and you change your life.

What fits your niche/product/offer/personal brand?

Social media channels should fit you well, like your favorite jeans. Now sometimes those jeans fit great right off the shelf, but other times you've got to work them in and after time they become your go-to pair.

For me, Twitter is a perfect fit. (Even though I had to work in it a while to find out.) It works extremely well for what I consider to be my niches – training, speaking, writing, consulting, and coaching.

Do you know your niche? This is very important. It's NOT network marketing. That's like saying Amazon's niche is online sales. You have to dig deeper.

I'm a speaker and a trainer and a coach, but more specifically, I'm a promoter and a connector. I'm a lid-lifter. I like to experience people's stories and lives on a granular level. I want to view your website and read your blogs. Go through your best tweets. Promote what you do and how you do it. I want to help people be great. I want to mentor and push them to accomplish their big goals and dreams. Twitter works for me for all of this.

To determine what works for you, you first need to understand your niche(s), your product, your personality, and your personal brand. And don't forget that we all could use a fresh audience or even a rebirth sometimes.

Who is your target audience and where do they congregate?

Two of the most important questions to ask yourself as you determine your unique approach to social media: Who is your target audience? Where do they hang out? Chris Freytag says, "People can get overwhelmed when it comes to choosing what to use. Figure out where your industry goes - where are your customers/fans/people to connect with? Go there."

Target audience is tricky, but you must determine who it is. If you're like 80% or more of networkers I've worked with, you will say that your target market is everyone. WRONG. This is too broad to tackle.

Determine who your ideal customer and business partner is and go where they go. If your product is very visual, like jewelry or merchandise of some sort, Pinterest and Instagram can be ideal. If your product is an online, web, or software solution, YouTube might be better to find people who enjoy technical products. If your product is skin care, definitely consider Pinterest, which attracts a lot of women. If you represent nutritional products or you are heavily focused on the business aspect, consider Twitter for meeting business-minded people. Twitter is great for sharing nutrition tips, links, and information. Of course, Facebook works great for most niches.

If your products lend themselves to great recipes or your merchandise looks great in pictures, consider Pinterest. However, if your goal is to meet more business minded men, Pinterest is probably not going to do it (it's predominantly used by women). Twitter is great for fast paced conversations, but if you hate writing and want to use a lot of images and photos, Twitter probably won't work.

You can do yourself a HUGE favor by narrowing your target market to determine how to streamline your message and use social media to connect. You can always expand your target demographic later, but if you start with too wide of a group or too many types of people, you'll end up missing your potential. No one wants to be an underachiever. You are in this to win it, so think like a business person and marketer. Let's narrow down your target.

APPLICATION:

1. What type of social media is attractive to you? Visual like Pinterest or Instagram? Short writing like Twitter? A written blog or creating videos? As you learn more about the options available to you, ask what your instinct is saying.
2. Who is your target market? Let's get nitty gritty. Narrow it down to one specific person – their age, sex, income bracket, likes, fears, aspirations, etc. Once you really drill down, you can expand from there.
3. Where is your target market? If you're marketing jewelry, skin care, or cosmetics, a visual channel might work best. If you work with nutritional products, maybe a more informational site would work.
4. Who do you want to meet? Where are these people hanging out on social media? What sites? Ask questions and do a little research.

SECTION 4: YOUR STOP PITCHING & START CONNECTING STRATEGY

The world is moving into a value-driven economy that thrives on connection.

Think about it. Some of the most popular products available today are either free, or they allow you to have a choice over what you consume. Almost everything you would ever need to research can be found for free on Google. Instructions for virtually every project, challenge, or repair can be located using YouTube. A subscription to Netflix or Amazon Prime allows you to watch television and movies on your schedule, without advertisements.

Movements and communities are being built from this new value-based economy. Yelp users have formed a tight, growing group who connect through common experiences. Trip Advisor users pick entire vacations on the feedback from reviewers they trust. People are finding value and sharing it with others in ways never before possible.

Businesses and entrepreneurs who embrace and perpetuate this movement will be rewarded. Evidence is all around you. Old models of doing business are dying rapidly or playing catchup because they have to.

Think about ways you can add your unique value to the world. You know it's not through selling and pitching. It's through connecting and lifting others up. By giving away value you create a vacuum that likes to be filled. It can work like a magnet. Embrace it. You have a lot to offer the world, so don't hold back!

Before we delve into the specific social media channels available and what works best for you, let's talk big picture strategy. No matter what social channel(s) you choose, the concepts in this section are key to your success. You may want to refer back to this section after you choose the social media channel(s) you're going to make your own. For now, get the general concepts in place so you can apply them as you read the rest of this book.

CHAPTER 8: HAVE A GOAL – BE PURPOSEFUL

"Three words of advice: Interact, promote, and enjoy!" –Lydia Aswolf-Carey

I find many people (including networkers) jump into social media for business without ever having a goal. Hard to believe, but it's true.

Without a strategy, without goals or even a singular goal, you are like a ship on the ocean with no compass. Even worse – you don't have a destination.

"Define your goal. Before you get started, develop a plan for how you're going to accomplish what it is you're setting out to do with varied and useful content that makes others want to follow you," says Lydia Aswolf-Carey.

Possibly worse than having no strategy at all is the goal of making money through social media. I've worked with hundreds of people who looked at social media as a golden goose, just waiting for you to collect her priceless eggs.

I've seen networkers spend 30, 60, or 90 days clinging to this idea, thinking they were tapping into an endless ATM. Then they get discouraged. They abandon their efforts altogether, become horribly inconsistent, or use social media as their latest time waster and way to avoid taking action towards their business goals.

I strongly urge you to have a weekly strategy meeting with yourself regarding your social media goals and presence. Some people have it every other week or monthly, but I highly recommend weekly.

I hold mine every Sunday evening before I go to bed. Here's what I do:

- I decide what I want to accomplish. For me, it's almost always the same three pieces: 1) I want to put out content that adds value to people's lives 2) I want to promote great people and what they're up to 3) I want to network and connect (and reconnect) with like-minded people.

- My main focuses are Twitter and my blog.
- I use Hootsuite to schedule about 50-70% of my tweets for the week.
- I brainstorm blog topics for my blog(s). If I'm feeling particularly inspired, I will write the blog that night. If not, I've got some topics to work from and will finish it on Monday or Tuesday.
- Next, I review the Notifications section of my Twitter account, looking for people I need to connect with or thank.
- I'm not terribly concerned with numbers of followers, retweets, or subscribers. You might be, and that is okay. For me, it's about quality, not quantity. So I look for what was retweeted. What did people respond to? What did I tweet that caused more people to follow me? I want to do more of that.
- I also use a tool called Twimemachine.com to review past tweets. There is nothing wrong with reusing content, especially if it fits into your strategy.
- I spend about 10 minutes writing content for tweets and a little blog promotion.
- I spend about 5 minutes scheduling tweets to promote other people, blogs, books, etc.
- Next I determine how I can best network that week. A tweetchat maybe? A live event? Possibly something on Facebook? It could be as simple as reaching out to someone who follows me to find out more about what they do. It could be interviewing someone for my Limitless series of blogs. You get the picture.
- I also make it a point to spend 15-20 minutes a day on Twitter and Facebook to post live, connect, retweet, and see what's going on in people's lives and businesses.

Keep your strategy simple, but HAVE A STRATEGY! Use the free strategy session guide at StopPitching.com/resources if you need some help.

With 100,000 Twitter followers and a thriving coaching, speaking, and mentoring career, Steve Gutzler has to make the best use of his time and energy to capitalize on social media. Here are the questions Steve asks himself each week:

1. What am I building? Basic question. I want a network of collaborators with high trust for me.
2. What's my purpose, why do I even exist out there, why am I throwing my hat in the ring? For me, it's three things: positive influence, impacting people for good, and trying to inspire greatness in individuals. There are a lot of people trying to do that, but I feel like I'm hitting the mark with it. I've had people approach me. It's **referabilty.**
3. What are the results I'm going to measure? How many tweets a day, goals regarding followers, social media platforms, etc. I'd like to master?
4. I come up with action plans. Every weekend, either Friday or Saturday I write my tweets for one full week. I have it all planned out. I add additional things I want to work on. Lean and mean, in and out quick. I focus on high value, otherwise it's diluted and ineffective.

Simple, right? Steve knows his stuff. And notice that 'selling' was nowhere in the mix.

Your strategy will change. You will adapt it, grow it, maybe even scrap it and start anew. All of that is okay and to be expected. But you will NEVER get the results you're looking for if you don't know what you're looking for and you don't create a road map to get there.

APPLICATION:

1. Set a time and day for your weekly strategy session.
2. If you need a little help, use the free Strategy Session Guide at StopPitching.com/resources to help you craft a weekly session that works for you.

3. Adapt and modify your session and strategy as you learn and grow. Trust the process!

CHAPTER 9: CONTENT IS KING

"Create content that people can't live without." —Cliff Ravenscraft, known as the Podcast Answer Man and founder of the Generally Speaking Production Network. He has helped thousands of people launch successful podcasts.

In every interview I did with social media experts, providing great content was mentioned in some way. Creating and posting solid content is a proven, long-term tactic to connect with others and attract people to your online platform.

That sounds like a no-brainer, but what does great content look like?

According to Lydia Aswolf-Carey, one aspect of good content is making sure it is varied and useful. Her comments go back to our earlier chapter on creating a consistent strategy session with yourself. "Before you get started, develop a plan for how you're going to accomplish what it is you're setting out to do with varied and useful **content** that makes others want to follow you. Don't rely on the same tired old content every hour, day, week, and month. You need to mix up your content to increase your followers, get leads, make conversions, and have a good time chatting with great people while doing so!"

I've seen this area stump many. "Alex," they say, "I don't have any good content." This is nonsense. All of us are full of useful, valuable content. It surrounds us in everyday life.

Remember your niches we talked about before? You want great content that comes from or connects to those places. It goes back to one of the main concepts of this book—focusing on our big WHY, the passion behind how we live our lives, the goals of our inner person. When we do this, we more easily start connecting with people because content comes naturally and with authenticity.

"It is very important to create content for others in a powerful way that enables and invites connection," says Geoff Talbot. "Engagement is guaranteed when we can take all our attention off ourselves."

JB Glossinger further advises, "The real thing is just being authentic and putting a lot of content out there. I think where people get into trouble is when they don't put content out. You've got to be consistent."

Tracey Ehman, an online presence and social media strategist, agrees. "That's the secret formula: consistency, being very relevant, and creating content and value that's attractive."

Sounds simple enough, right?

One challenge is when you are trying to post content about your business, your company, or your products. That's only a fraction of your strategy, not your strategy. I highly encourage you to focus on the **90/10 rule** with this.

The 90/10 Rule

The 90/10 rule is simple – make 90% of your posts about connecting, promoting others, sharing great content, engaging in conversations, and adding value. The remaining 10% can be about promoting your blog, your products, your business, or anything else you want to market.

This rule is not strict or exact. You might find 80/20 works for you or something in between. However, until you find a method and formula that works well for you, err on the side of 10% or less when it comes to promoting.

Many people will adhere to an 80/20 balance, but I prefer to stay closer to 90/10. Why? It's worked for me. It's what I've seen working for others. It's what successful people have advised me to do.

I've seen a lot of networkers fail at this by making their posts 50/50 or even 80% selling, pitching, and promoting, instead of what really works. Don't fall into that trap.

"If someone is saying, 'join me, join me, join me,' all the time, you either do or you don't and then stop following that person," Jamie Stewart points out. "If someone is posting great content, you are more likely to follow them – the 90/10 rules applies, 90% good, entertaining info, 10% about what you sell."

When I asked Bruce Van Horn what percentage of his tweets promoted his books, website, and offers, he said, "It's about 10%. I like Gary Vaynerchuk's book *Jab, Jab, Jab, Right Hook*. I say give, give, give, then ask."

The 90/10 rule is simple – make 90% of your posts about value, content, fun, and promoting others, and 10% promoting you, your products, your site, or your business.

Kill the jargon

If you're following the 90/10 rule, what do you say when you do promote yourself, your offer, your products, or your business? Great question. Let's start with what NOT say.

Stay away from the network marketing and direct sales jargon. Words like downline, upline, commissions, unilevel, etc., can immediately make people feel weird or have them shy away from you before you ever make contact.

Instead of using a bunch of industry or company jargon, be human. Talk in your voice. Be real. Talk about **benefits**. Use stories. Tap into emotion. Remember, we want to connect, not pitch or chase people away.

Here is some magical advice: create curiosity.

If someone is interested in what you do, then you'll have plenty of time to drop the jargon on them. Until then, stay away from it. Be a conversationalist instead.

You're already an expert

Another challenge is when you think you have to be a business expert, motivational speaker, or social media maven in order to create content that people care about. This is simply not true. Your content should come from what you know and what you are passionate about.

If creating content consistently is holding you back, relax. You just need enough to get started and gain a little traction. Pick something that you are familiar with, have experience in, and like. Try to make it somewhat applicable to what you offer in your business, but this isn't entirely necessary. It's more important to find something you can create regularly, that will add value to people's lives.

If you're an expert at hiking, then post about that. Tips. Advice. Experiences. How-to information. News about hiking. Reviews of trails. Mistakes you've made and how to avoid them. Be good at what you're good at! When you are putting out great content, consistently, the right people will find you.

Please don't try to be someone you're not. This is when content is hard to create and it becomes hollow. Great relationships are at the heart of almost every business. Relationships are built on trust and genuineness. If you try to be someone you're not, people will eventually see right through you.

The same principle applies to your business and your online brand. If you try to be someone you're not, it won't work. If you try to impress people instead of help people, it won't work. If you try to build a strategy that allows you to trap people like a spider's web so you can pitch them, it won't work.

Your content is a big extension of you. And just like your life, your content will evolve and change over time. Just because you're posting about hiking today doesn't mean you won't be blogging about living the life of your dreams later.

You want to be known for something. This means your content should mostly fall into a few categories. You can post interesting content on a wide variety of topics, but try to keep 50-75% of your strategy around one or two content areas. (Again, think about those niches we talked about in an earlier chapter. What are YOUR niches?)

If you saw someone post pregnancy tips this morning, football news at noon, and travel advice at night, you might find some of it useful, but they won't be someone you will follow. If someone blogs about their kids today, investment tips tomorrow, and how to build a picnic bench the next week, you don't know what's coming next.

Consistency doesn't just mean posting regularly; it means defining and developing your personal brand. People want to know what to expect. When you're consistent, it makes you attractive, and people will want to connect with you. Win!

One area to avoid: always talking about yourself. While your family and some friends may like this, ultimately it won't attract new people if you only discuss number one. Definitely include insights and experiences, but mundane details or conceited posts won't get you very far.

Content strategy tips:

Adjust your goals and adapt your strategy as you go along. You will find things that work and do more of them, while at the same time find that parts of your strategy fall flat and ditch them.

Avoid growing impatient and resorting to pitching, selling, and chasing. It's no fun and it won't work long term.

Do not give up, ever. Building your online platform and social media presence will take time.

Stay away from being judgmental, abusive, curt, political, or religious. Stay true to your convictions, but let your actions be your mantra, not your words.

Never be divisive. If someone is rude to you or says something negative about you, ignore them. Easier said than done, I know. But very important. Take the high road.

Repurposing, sharing, and promoting are all good, but never steal or plagiarize.

Be yourself. Your strategy, above all, should share the unique you. Your passions, struggles, story, experiences, expertise, and humility. People connect and follow people, not facts or details. Share your vision!

Remember that your personal brand is everything you post, at all times. That picture of you staggering drunk or that harsh political rant can be seen by potential business partners. Not everything was meant to be shared!

APPLICATION:

1. What are one or two content areas or topics you can regularly post about? Think about your passion, experiences, and life in general.
2. Example – I like to post about speaking, gratitude, and sales strategies. I post tips, advice, and blog articles. What do you see yourself posting with consistency?
3. Think about this and let it seep into your brain. You don't have to have all the answers right now. Next chapter we will get into what you can do with these topics.

CHAPTER 10: CONTENT IDEAS

Stumped for content ideas or need a little help? Here's a list of suggestions to get your brain in motion:

Interviews can generate a lot of interest, and they don't have to be lengthy. This is a great way to meet new people as well. When you interview someone, you are promoting them and their business, book, website, blog, etc. This gives you the opportunity to meet a wide range of people.

Pain points are another great area of content. What is your target market's needs? What do they hate? What are their hopes, goals, and dreams? What are their passions? Tips, experiences, advice, and stories can attract an audience.

Related topics. For example, if your product line revolves around jewelry, handbags, or clothing, post about fashion. If your products have to do with nutrition or wellness, post weight loss, fitness, or health tips.

Lists work well. A list of great books on your favorite topic or your favorite recipes or your most useful ways to accomplish something. Lists are easy to digest, understand, and take action on. They can also be strung out over many posts to get more mileage and consistency.

How-to posts are extremely popular and work well both in writing and video. Useful instructions also work because people will refer back to them and they will look at you as an expert who provided great value.

Mistakes and how to avoid them are helpful and show humility. I'm not talking about extreme errors or that mistake that got you fired when you were in high school. No, I mean showing your experience and maturity by talking about a mistake and how to help others not do the same.

Personal stories of triumph can be winners. Use these sparingly and be brief when you do. Make sure your audience can relate to them as well. Create empathy. Everyone has challenges to overcome, so sharing how you triumphed can win people over.

Observe life around you. Stories and content are happening everywhere. I once wrote two blogs and over a dozen tweets from spending 30 minutes in Starbucks. Keep your mind open and alert and great content could find you.

Reviews. This is pretty self-explanatory. Think products, services, websites, blogs, books, etc.

Promote others. If you read a great blog, promote it. If you use a great business or product, promote it. Like what someone is up to, promote them. If you do this, make sure you do it in a genuine way with no personal agenda.

A mix of third party content. I regularly post links to blogs, articles, videos, and information I find useful. When someone discovers great information on another website because of you, it adds to your credibility.

APPLICATION:

1. Now that I've given you some ideas, how can you apply them to your topics of content from last chapter? Brainstorm what ideas you would like to utilize.
2. If something excites you, chase that feeling. Passion is critical to creating great content.
3. Schedule time each week to brainstorm content, or create a way to keep notes when you have good ideas so you can come back to them.
4. Have fun when creating content! You're sharing your expertise and passion. Your experience could impact someone in a very profound way.

CHAPTER 11: ADDING VALUE

*"The biggest thing for me, it's how I live my life, what can I do for others? It's about **adding value"**.*-Lolly Daskal, listed as one of the top 100 thought leaders to follow in business.

Above all, your social media and digital marketing strategy should be based around adding value to the world. Give your target market something they can chew on. Adding value helps you reach people who aren't interested in what you have to offer right now, but they might be someday. Even more so, they may be interested simply because it's you.

There are many times in our lives when we do something not because it's the best price or the highest quality, we do it because we like the person involved. When someone adds value to your life it hits the subconscious and stays there. You can probably remember times in your life when people were nice to you for no reason, gave you the royal treatment when they didn't have to, or went out of their way to help you accomplish something.

Like JB Glossinger says, "You're going to find people that will follow you and listen to you if you bring value into their lives."

A story about adding value

My first trip to San Diego with my young family happened in 2001. I was so happy to be able to afford to take them to this beautiful city and spend time at the beach. We went there for a wedding and decided to stay a few days afterward to enjoy the sun and fun.

Wouldn't you know it, right as we pulled up to the beach, our vehicle died. I mean dead as a doornail stopped running and broke down.

My wife, being the always positive force in our family, grabbed our three kids and headed to the sand while I called for a tow.

A little while later, a very dirty, tired tow truck driver showed up. Said he had been working 24 straight hours. He asked me where I wanted to take my van for service. I told him I did not know the area, so the closest dealership would have to suffice.

I have to admit I was a little nervous. The tow truck driver, by all appearances, was sketchy. He said to me, "The dealership? They're going to screw you over. Let me take it to my guy. Get in."

Nervous? No, I was downright scared.

As he drove me to 'his guy,' I prayed the entire drive. Luckily, it was only about 10 minutes, but that was 10 minutes of feverish prayer.

We showed up to a repair shop that was small, but very busy. A man came out and talked with the driver. The tow truck driver relayed my situation, explaining that I was from out of town and broke down at the beach.

I thought I was being fed to the wolves. Easy prey. But I was wrong.

The mechanic introduced himself as Troy, the owner. He took one look at my vehicle and said it most likely had a broken timing belt. He then promised he would move it up in line and have it done before close. It was already into the afternoon. I was stunned.

He also said the tow truck driver would give me a ride back to the beach, and to call him when we were ready to be picked up so he could take us to our hotel.

Unreal!

I called a taxi instead of asking Troy to pick us up at the beach. When he called to let me know our car was ready, he seemed annoyed that we took a cab. I told him it was no problem, and I'd take a cab to the repair shop.

"That's stupid," he said. "I'm on my way."

He picked me up at my hotel, gave me a deep discount on the repair bill, and told me to enjoy the rest of my vacation.

Now that's value in the best way.

Years later, when I moved to San Diego from Phoenix, can you guess where I took my cars for repair work? You got it – Mission Bay Automotive, Troy's shop. You never forget when someone provides awesome service or value. People are loyal to you and want to send you more business. I've referred everyone I know to Troy.

That's the power of giving away great value without an agenda. And it can work for you and your business too.

APPLICATION:

1. Adding value to others means giving them your best. Going back to your content ideas, what can you do that adds value to someone's daily life?
2. You don't have to give away great value all of the time. Value can be delivered in many ways, like referring someone, connecting two people, or promoting someone's offer. Who can you refer or connect to add value?
3. What tips and advice from your life and experiences can you share with others on a regular basis?
4. To be a difference maker, you only need to impact one person. Your strategy does not have to reach millions, just the right people. When you craft content, think quality over quantity.

CHAPTER 12: CONSISTENCY IS KEY

"Consistency is the key – don't give up on it." – Chris Freytag

I have already said a lot about consistency, but I want to drill it into your head even more. Creating your platform requires showing up, even when no one else does. Many people are just waiting to see if you stick around. People don't want to put their valuable time into building a relationship with you if you're here today, gone tomorrow.

Reliability is a commodity that's become scarce in today's fast-paced, online world. A big part of winning the battle is simply being reliable. Posting every day. Commenting every day. Doing what you say you're going to do.

Whatever you decide – Facebook, Twitter, blogging, Instagram, Pinterest – do it consistently. You can evolve your content and strategy over time (and trust me, you will), but be engaged regularly.

In our microwave, instant gratification society, it's easy to throw in the towel after a few weeks or months. I've seen countless people dive into a new social media channel and give up after a few weeks. "It doesn't work," they will say. Nothing works when you give up on it. If it were easy and instantaneous, everyone would be an overnight, online superstar.

"Chip away and be consistent," says Steve Gutzler. "Social media is just one slice of who I am and my personal brand. It keeps me fresh and vibrant. It's kind of cool that someone can go from corporate role to entrepreneur and be seen that way on social media."

I cannot say it (or write it) enough. You must have a marathon approach with consistency at its core. "The ONLY way for social media to work is to be consistent," according to Luke Dancy.

APPLICATION:

1. Make a commitment that you're going to implement a social media strategy that you can work consistently. Don't over extend yourself or make promises you can't keep. Even if you start slow, just start and be consistent.

CHAPTER 13: SUBTLE MARKETING

As I've already stated, we are firmly in the connection economy. Permission marketing is the key to long-term growth and success. Endless salesmanship and pitching will drive people away from you and make you say "social media doesn't work."

I want to be very, very clear about this. The connection economy means sales when you truly connect. Revenue built through trust and relationships. Permission marketing means you have earned the right to market to someone. They trust you, like what you're all about, and want more of what you have to offer.

Part of your social media strategy is most definitely to get more prospects into your funnel, more customers buying your products, and to find potential business partners. However, this will come as a result of what you do to *earn* those opportunities. Don't worry about how it's going to happen, just trust this process.

Think about it like this. When people start a network marketing business, they usually have a few people they know join or buy from them. These are people in their current network who already trust them. As they grow their business, the number one challenge I hear from networkers is that they run out of warm market and people to talk to. They resort to buying leads, placing ads, or working trade shows. This is NOT what they signed up to do!

Now imagine an endless resource to build your warm market. Imagine a funnel that grew each and every month. The more consistent you are, the more strategic you are, and the more you connect, the bigger your funnel.

Imagine the same person starting a network marketing business with three or four times the number of trusted relationships. It would probably result in double (or more) the number of prospects, customers, and business partners they enrolled.

By reading this book, you're on to something. It's hard work, so most people won't do it. But you will.

"Social media requires a very different approach than direct marketing. The worst thing any company or individual can do is be too direct in trying to sell their services or products on social media. Learn to think of social media as subtle marketing," advises social media manager Lydia Aswolf-Carey.

I love that term – **subtle marketing**. It describes the **Stop Pitching, Start Connecting strategy** almost perfectly. Subtle, passive marketing will take you farther than any up front, in your face promoting.

Picture a room with 100 people in it. You get to pitch your business. You might get 10 interested. Of those, maybe three will actually buy. The end result, most likely, will be that one will stick around, maybe buy for a few months, and maybe refer one person. Then you start the cycle all over again.

Now picture giving all 100 people something of great value. They appreciate you. Some level of trust is instantly gained. Now you present to them. Your percentages of success automatically go up. Instead of three buying from you, you will get seven to 10 of them to buy.

Finally, imagine the same 100 people, but you give them consistent value over time. They constantly see you as a positive resource. They jump in and read your blog a few times a month. You give them a tip that helps them be a better parent or make better health decisions. They see you as a solutions person. A few months later it hits them: they would love to create residual income or a home-based business, but they don't know where to start.

BOOM!

Because you have connected, built trust, and been consistent, they contact you. Victory my friends!

APPLICATION:

1. Go a week without presenting or pitching on social media. Instead, put out great content and add value. Start with the 100/0 rule – 100% great content and value with zero selling on social networking.
2. Engage with others. Join the conversation. Comment and like posts. Do it genuinely.
3. Promote someone you like or a product you use. Share a link to a great article or book. Connect two people you know who don't know each other.
4. If you're someone who has never promoted your business or products using social media because you don't know what to say, that's okay. Start by creating some curiosity this week by posting great content that relates to your offer. For example, you are working with nutritional products, post a few third party articles about the benefits of specific ingredients found in your products.

CHAPTER 14: THE MARATHON APPROACH

"It's a marathon, not a sprint. We are still at the beginning of social media. Every week something new is coming out. You can't do it all, so think of it as a marathon race." –Luke Dancy

This is another area I hope I have drilled into your brain – the marathon approach. Give your online brand at least one year to develop. Commit to using a new social media channel for 12 months before you say it doesn't work and give up.

I worked with an owner who made giving up a sport. He never gave any project time to grow wings. Why? He was always looking for the magic bullet. He was convinced that overnight success could truly happen overnight. It's almost as if he believed in unicorns and mermaids.

I implemented programs and promotions that resulted in the three highest months of new sales volume in company history. They happened separately, in part because we never followed through on any initiative.

After launching a road show that produced an incredible sales month, I was asked how we follow it up. "Easy," I told him, "Another road show. Let's do it every month." However, he was looking for a brand new idea.

When I explained that it was consistency we needed, his thirst for the magic bullet could not be quenched. He was not happy when I told him we would not have the same explosive results, but we'd get the growth we were looking for over time. We never did another road show, and the momentum we built died within 60 days.

A blockbuster movie usually has its best sales on opening weekend, right? Rarely can you duplicate the magic and luster of that first release weekend. In fact, if you're like me, you will wait until it's been in theaters for a month, and then go see it. By that time, you will see the movie with the theater 25% full, when just a month ago that same movie was sold out.

How does the movie continue to be a 'box office' success? DVD sales. People watching on Netflix or Amazon Prime. Theater releases in other countries. Merchandise sales. A marathon, long term strategy can make it a winner. In fact, many movies that bomb in theaters go on to be financially successful because they have consistent marketing over the long haul.

This is how you need to think about your business, your personal brand, your online platform, and your social media strategy: the marathon approach.

APPLICATION:

1. Commit to at least one year of consistency. No matter what social media channels you take on, make a commitment that you will stick with them for at least 12 months.
2. Consider making a contract with yourself that you actually sign and put on a calendar. A year later review your forward progress and have a big idea strategy session with yourself to see how you've grown, what you did well, and where your opportunities lie. Maybe you'll even want to add something new!
3. Consider this commitment when mulling over your options on social media. If you dread writing, do not start a written blog. You'll never keep your commitment. Pick something you will enjoy doing so consistency will happen organically.

CHAPTER 15: TIME MANAGEMENT

*"Budget your time. Time manage your social media. I might go in once a day and spend 15 minutes to answer questions. I could spend that time watching television, but I use it to **connect** with people."* -Chris Freytag.

One of the big myths about social media is that it takes too much time, or people who use it are wasting a lot of time. Like any good thing, there are people who are going to abuse it. You probably know someone who spends hours on Facebook posting selfies, memes, quotes, and survey results letting you know what 80's movie they belong in. Possibly even people you've worked with or people in your organization.

There are people who drink too much wine, and then there are wine makers who are artists. There are prescriptions that save lives, and then there are people who take them like candy.

Do not let a few bad apples spoil your image of what social media can do. The key is to be efficient. You need to manage your time and you can do this through your strategy. Strategic use of social media should NOT take a lot of time.

"Social media is brilliant for letting people make use of pockets of time," explains Jamie Stewart. "Think about the things you want to share, and write them down somewhere, so when you have time you have things to share."

A strategy is critical so you can maximize your time. By being deliberate, you will focus on what really matters and what produces results in the form of growing your connections and ultimately your business.

Lisha Yost, a self-made entrepreneur with a social media management business called Twonder Woman, advises, "Don't waste time on things that don't matter. Only do what will get you results. Humans typically spend 20% of their time on things that matter, and 80% of their time on things that really won't do anything for them in the long run. Try to switch that so that you're spending most of your efforts on doing things that will get you results. And think **long term.** What can you do now that will get you recurring results later?"

I call it results-driven activity, or RDA for short. Are you focusing on the activities that produce results? As an network marketer, a large percentage of your time must be focused on prospecting, inviting, and presenting. But some of your time should be focused on putting more people into your funnel, and that's where a strategic approach comes in.

The last thing I want you to do is spend the next 90 days focusing only on social media, blogging, email marketing, etc. Because the Stop Pitching strategy is a marathon approach, time management is essential. Being diverse with your networking is also essential.

My good friend and MLM philosopher David Colister calls it "rocking chair activity" – you can rock that baby all day and you're not going anywhere.

Time management tips

- Set a specific time each week to review the week prior and create your strategy/posts/tweets/blogs/etc. for the upcoming week.
- Find time for using social media regularly. If you're struggling to find focused time, cut something else out. Carve out 20 minutes to work on your platform.
- Set a time limit on your daily social media. I like to get on for 15-20 minutes while I eat breakfast, 10 minutes around lunch, and 15 minutes after my kids are in bed. I've created a routine that works for me, and you should too. This way you can avoid falling into the trap of wasting time on social media or going days without checking in.
- Make time for engagement. Posting your content is good, but engaging with others is what it's all about. Respond to posts. Retweet others. Comment. Share. Repin. Promote people. Thank people when they promote you.

- Keep your eyes on the long-term prize. Stay honed in on the goal of connecting and growing your warm market.

APPLICATION:

1. Carve out time for connecting and implementing your strategy. Look through your calendar and schedule the time.
2. Create a daily routine or schedule you can stick to. Make sure you are getting on social media each day.
3. What can you cut out of your daily schedule to make more time to connect with people?
4. How will you make sure you don't waste time on things that don't matter?

CHAPTER 16: APPS – YOU'VE GOT TO HAVE THEM

All of the social networking sites I've discussed have free mobile/smartphone apps. These apps make it super easy to check your account and post from anywhere. It's especially useful to get alerts and notifications on your phone when you don't have time to be in front of a computer.

Phone apps can help you employ a good time management strategy. Instead of taking time away from an important task (like prospecting or follow up), you can jump on social media while extra time presents itself.

For example, if you're waiting in a long line, check your social media channels and engage. If you're on public transportation or a long car ride (and not driving), plug into social media on your phone.

Some social networks, like Instagram, cannot be effectively used without the phone app.

I love that I can check Twitter and Facebook from almost anywhere. It allows me to connect or respond more quickly and share photos and updates almost instantly.

People can get annoyed with these apps because of all of the alerts available. I admit that when I got a new phone, the bombardment of notifications was a bit overwhelming. However, all of these notifications can be turned on or off, so tap into this customization to personalize your social networking experience on your phone.

Bottom line – apps make life easier, especially business and connecting. You've got to have them.

APPLICATION:

1. Do you have phone apps for the social networks you're using? If not, download them right now.
2. Start using these apps when you're out and about. Maximize any free time you might have to connect with people via social networking.
3. If you don't have a phone that allows these types of applications, please consider upgrading as soon as possible. Most carriers have fantastic deals to help you get started.

PART II: DIGGING INTO YOUR OPTIONS

You've got the mindset for social media. You're equipped with the strategy to make it work for you. But where to begin? The second half of *Start Pitching and Start Connecting* goes into detail about social media options and why they may (or may not) work for you.

As you read, ask yourself the questions we explored in previous chapters about which channel is the best fit for your personality, passion, and the business you want to market. Think about the strategies and how they would apply to each channel. You may want to skim all of your options, then choose a social media option to start with. After you've made your choice, read that specific chapter more slowly and take the time to work through the application steps at the end of each chapter.

You may already be interacting with some of these channels. Think about how you can improve your effectiveness and adapt your strategy. Or maybe there is a channel you no longer see as a fit. That's perfectly fine - let it go!

This is where it starts to get fun my friends. We've covered the big picture. Like shopping at your favorite store, now it's time to go through your options and make informed decisions to establish your platform.

SECTION 5: TWITTER

Hearing the buzz, I joined Twitter in 2009 to see what it was all about. I tweeted a few times, sporadically. I followed a few people. I didn't get it. It seemed like a waste of time or something that simply wasn't for me. I couldn't make sense of it. I abandoned it. Any of this sound familiar? You may have felt the same way.

After a few friends talked about finding new connections on Twitter and said I would love the people I met there, I gave it another try in January 2011. This time I was determined to get it. Nothing was going to stop me from understanding it and using it effectively this time.

I had some help from a friend and also jumped into free training on Mashable.com. I was off and running.

At first, when I started to follow some higher profile social media people, my home feed was flooded with tweets from just a few people. Immediately I wanted to throw in the towel because I reverted back to those old thoughts. I thought it was a waste of time or that I would never understand it.

I fought these thoughts off with my determination to learn. When I hit a road block, I asked for help. I wasn't afraid to ask other people on Twitter or to run to my friend Google for an answer. Things like:

- How many people should I follow per day?
- How often should I tweet?
- How do I determine a content strategy for Twitter?
- What mistakes are people making?
- How do I get retweeted? (And so on.....)

Things started clicking when I followed a few local people in San Diego. These were professional, like-minded individuals I'd never met before. You know what? I never would have met them without Twitter. That's when the light bulb went off.

There are thousands, if not millions of people on Twitter who I can meet and connect with. People looking to network with people like me, who I would NEVER meet otherwise.

And that, my friends, is the biggest benefit I see to being active and effective on Twitter. Access to an incredible pool of people who you would never be able to access in any other location. Quality over quantity.

I know what some of you are thinking, "Sure Alex, you can meet like-minded associates on Twitter, but that won't result in real relationships." This is simply not true. I'm living proof.

Not only have I found outstanding people to connect with on Twitter, I've taken many of these connections to the next level. I've had calls with them. I've met them in person, eaten meals with them, hiked with them. I've involved them in projects. I've been interviewed by them. I've referred them. I've interviewed them for this book.

Twitter works, and I believe it is the one of the best social channels for expanding your network.

I think almost every social media site can add value to you and your business, but only a few of them will actually lead you to NEW people in your life. Twitter has worked for me.

In the next section we'll explore the other social media options, but because Twitter is such a powerful tool for entrepreneurs, I'm going to spend this whole section detailing effective use of this medium.

CHAPTER 17: HOW I USE TWITTER & WHY I LOVE IT

Of all the social media channels, Twitter is my favorite. Here's why: It's been an ideal place to connect with new people and grow my network.

If you are not on Twitter, or if you're not using it consistently, I encourage you to start. It's a great opportunity to round out your online platform and expand your warm market by thousands of people.

Don't think of Twitter as a recruiting tool or a place to sell, but rather a hallway with unlimited doors. Any one of these doors could turn into a connection that leads you to a thousand other connections.

When used in the right way, Twitter can be an extremely effective channel to develop your personal brand.

How I use Twitter

I use Twitter almost every day. With time, diligence, and consistency, I've developed a personal brand that has allowed me to meet many new people which has opened up opportunities on both sides.

I use Twitter to push out my passion – helping people realize they are limitless. I do this in a few ways:

I share business, sales, and marketing tips from my personal experience.

I post speaking tips on Twitter. I do this because I know that most of the world is petrified of public speaking. If I can help one person be more confident, take a chance, or polish their speaking skills, I know they will get more opportunities.

Often I post about inspirational topics that I personally find interesting or uplifting, including gratitude, leadership, and mindset.

I love to promote other people and their businesses or services. I only do this when I genuinely like or respect the person and what they're up to. When someone is doing great work, I want the rest of the world to know about it.

I retweet other people several times a day. I do this only with tweets or content I find valuable or worth sharing. I never retweet with any other agenda (it's tempting, but don't do it).

I also spend a few minutes each day connecting with people who have connected with me, tweeted great material, written a meaningful blog, or retweeted my tweets or blog. This is critical to anyone trying to grow their network. I feel like every minute I put into connecting on Twitter comes back to me double or more.

I promote my Limitless blogs where I interview people who have done extraordinary things. I also feature stories of people who have broken through limits, both external and self-imposed. I do this to inspire people to break through their own obstacles and realize that being limitless is an attitude and state of mind. By writing and sharing a topic I'm extremely passionate about, people not only get inspired, but they see the real me. This attracts like-minded people.

Are you seeing a trend yet? So far, I haven't mentioned how often I sell on Twitter. I haven't told you that each day I try to pitch, sell, or make money through Twitter. No way.

My strategy is simple: give away great value, be consistent, connect, and be genuine. You may want to write those four things down, in your own words, and make them your mantra. This book could literally be summed up with those four statements.

It's not just me that lives by these words. As you've probably noticed so far, the social media and business experts I interviewed, people in my network, are going to tell you the same thing in their own words.

Why is Twitter so effective?

It's fast paced. As you start following lots of people, tweets really get moving. It may seem too fast at first, but in today's society quick is the reality. Conversations happen very quickly, and you can make a lot of progress in just a few minutes. An hour is an eternity on Twitter.

It's short. 140 characters short. Many people have a short attention span, so the brevity of tweets works well for this. It sharpens your writing and marketing skills because you must be brief. I can look over 20 or more tweets from one user in a matter of seconds, seeing what they are all about. I can click on their name, see their links, website, picture, and bio in no time at all.

It's easy to follow new people, and unfollow people. I don't have to wait for someone to accept my request (in most cases) or follow me back. I can follow literally anyone. If I don't like their tweets I can unfollow them anytime. There are a lot of people who follow me, but I don't follow them. And on the reverse side, there are people I follow who do not follow me.

It attracts business-minded people. My Facebook account only contains my current network. When I meet new people that I like, I then connect with them on Facebook. But where do you meet new people? Twitter. I know I'm repeating this often, that's because I cannot stress it enough!

I've met entrepreneurs, social media experts, CEOs, coaches, business owners, authors, bloggers, writers, and people who run charitable organizations. They're everywhere. They use Twitter to spread the word and meet new people as well.

It's a community. It's a place people can go to get support, answers, and inspiration. Twitter users are very supportive of each other.

Features like lists, hashtags, and Twitter chats

Lists allow me to group the people I follow for easier tracking. I don't have to search for Steve Gutzler, Luke Dancy, or Lisha Yost on my home feed.

They're on one of my Twitter lists where I can easily scan what they're tweeting.

Hashtags are searchable terms people put in tweets that begin with the pound or hash sign. Like this: #StartConnecting or #Limitless. Hashtags become clickable links so you can see who else is using them. It's another layer of connection and meaning that is unique to Twitter. When used properly and consistently, they will help branding and draw new people to you. They will also help you find people and causes you want to support or connect with.

Twitter chats, or tweetchats, are fast-paced sessions that usually last an hour. Everyone participating will use the same hashtag term (i.e. #LeadFromWithin) when responding to a series of questions. There are great websites to help facilitate these, both as a participant or if you want to hold your own Twitter chat. (They're not easy to follow on Twitter itself, but I will get into this later.) They are usually well orchestrated, so if you're thinking of an online chat room from 1998, it's nothing like that.

Why do I love Twitter chats? Each time I jump into one I gain a group of new followers and connections. I learn from their answers and interaction. These chat sessions draw in the like-minded like a magnet.

Easy to use management tools that work with Twitter. Hootsuite. JustUnfollow. Twubs. The list grows on and on. These sites and tools work extremely well with Twitter, turning it into a more effective networking weapon, not just a place to post pictures of your vacation or comment on current events.

What I like best about these tools is that they allow you to maximize your time. That's a big plus for me, and I'm sure for you too. Time is your most precious asset in life and as a businessperson. You can't afford to waste any of it. The tools that work with Twitter help you stay on top of your connecting game.

Twitter fits me like a glove. I'm passionate about using it (like you couldn't tell, right?). You may not feel the same way, but the more likely story is you just need to fully experience it. Sometimes things fit instantly, sometimes they take time.

My first pair of slip-on Vans shoes seemed tight. I didn't really like the color. However, they were a gift, so I gave them a shot. Over time, I grew to LOVE those shoes. I still own them today. They're beat up, faded, a little ugly, and they fit me like a glove.

Technology can fit like this. Twitter eventually did for me. At first it was too tight. Ugly. Wonky. Uncomfortable. It would have been easy to give up on it. Most great things in life take work and perseverance. So is the case for your social media skills, your personal brand, your online presence, and a Twitter account. Don't give up on it. If you want the best out of it, you have to give it your best.

APPLICATION:

1. What have you read so far that might make Twitter appealing to you? Make these part of your Twitter strategy.
2. What pieces of Twitter are you finding difficult to understand? Google these or ask Twitter users for help or why they use Twitter. You can also use the help feature on Twitter itself.
3. What could you share consistently on Twitter to help build your personal brand and online platform?

CHAPTER 18: WHY DO OTHERS LOVE TWITTER?

Author, blogger, and book reviewer Stacie Theis has built a fantastic social media presence and very popular blog in a short amount of time. Her network grew quickly through social media. She developed an identity and a meaningful business. By the way, Stacie is my wife.

Truth be told, there are days when I'm a little envious of what she's done. I'm also incredibly proud. Her hard work has turned into a business she can stand behind passionately.

Stacie is a work-from-home mom who was trying to find her vision and her passion. Of course, her top priorities, vision, passions, are her family, children, and household. But past that, she was looking for something to add value to the world. Something that was uniquely hers. Something meaningful where she could contribute and look forward to doing each day.

If you've struggled to use social media effectively for business, if you feel intimidated by Twitter, or if you are reluctant to get started, then this interview with Stacie is for you!

Alex: How did you get started on Twitter?

Stacie: I opened a Twitter account several years ago, but didn't understand how to use it and eventually gave up. A few years later I decided to create a website to help authors promote their books through interviews and reviews. I read a book regarding the importance of using social media, particularly Twitter, to promote yourself and your business. I decided Twitter was something I must learn to use effectively.

(The book Stacie read was *The Barefoot Executive* by Carrie Wilkerson)

Alex: What were your first few months like?

Stacie: I admit that Twitter was a bit intimidating at first with the different abbreviations and extensive use of hashtags. I discovered the best way to understand Twitter was to just dive right in and learn by trial and error. I found people to be friendly and eager to engage. By consistently tweeting and patiently learning I was able to quickly grasp the concept and become a tweeting pro.

Alex: How do you use Twitter?

Stacie: I use Twitter to make connections and meet prospective clients as well as to promote my business and my children's books.

Alex: Why do you like it?

Stacie: I like Twitter because people seem to be more genuine. They are always happy to help me spread the word on my reviews, interviews, and giveaways. Connecting with authors, publishers and other reviewers is essential to my business. Twitter makes networking with those specific individuals simple. The positive vibe and upbeat nature of Twitter is also something I enjoy.

Alex: How has Twitter helped you?

Stacie: Twitter has opened many doors for promoting and expanding my business, BeachBoundBooks. It has allowed me to network with many authors and reviewers, all of whom have played an important role in my rapid growth. When I released my children's books, my Twitter connections eagerly helped me spread the word. As an indie author, this has allowed me to sell far more copies than would have been possible without my social media presence.

Alex: What would you say to people who are reluctant to use Twitter?

Stacie: You will never learn new things unless you try. The benefits of using Twitter to promote yourself and your business are far too great an opportunity to miss out on. If you're unsure, start out slow with a few tweets a day, observe what others do, and make an effort to interact and follow new people. Soon you will feel comfortable enough to use Twitter as a path to reach your goals.

Why Twitter Works for Others

You know Stacie and I love Twitter. But don't just take our word for it. I've asked the experts why they love Twitter.

Luke Dancy: Twitter is like the rest of the world...it's fast paced, connected, and people are hooked to their cell phones anyway so you can get in touch with them almost any time of day.

Tracey Ehman: I use Twitter to keep my finger on the pulse of everything social media related, and love that I can favorite, reply, retweet or mention a post that I see as relevant to me and my clientele. I really like how easy it is to create rapport with less than 140 characters. The character limit actually forces you to be succinct in your posts and responses. I also like being able to easily search out topics and people I am interested in connecting with.

Lisha Yost: Twitter is simple, easy, fast, short (140 characters), and there are lots of Twitter tools to use like Hootsuite, Twitterfeed, and Tweetadder, just to name a few. Twitter is my favorite site for getting traffic to a blog because it's very information focused.

JB Glossinger: Twitter is one of my favorites because it's easy to communicate. When you become a resource...people come to you. It's like a great restaurant. People come to a great restaurant.

Osvaldo Blackaller (Chef Oz, local San Diego restaurant owner and avid social media user): I love Twitter because it has helped grow my business and connect with other humans around the globe. The best part of that is that I've met people in person through Twitter. As crazy as it sounds, I am thankful for the Twitter world because I can connect with people and minds alike. It allows us small business owners to take our in-house marketing to another level!

Bill Cortright: Understanding and implementing social media, especially Twitter, has changed my life and enhanced my career. Being in my early fifties, I didn't understand social media and its powerful reach. Gary

Vaynerchuk (author, speaker, and social media branding expert) actually gave me the best advice when I started: "Don't ask for anything. Build relationships and community." Twitter has connected my business in the last year in ways that would have taken me ten years in the past. Thousands of followers are engaged with me that I am proud to call my community. Twitter is a tool I use for collaboration and networking. (Bill is a speaker, entrepreneur, and personal trainer who has written several books and speaks on the topics of stress and diet.)

Lauren Galley: I love Twitter! My non-profit organization exploded with amazing mentors as I gained followers on this social media outlet. Unlike other social media outlets, Twitter has expanded my reach, and I find it easy to communicate with positive and like-minded people. I'm 19 and have over 11,000 followers. The most awesome part of my day is who I'm going to meet next! (Lauren is Founder and President of Girls Above Society, a non-profit organization that empowers teen girls to become confident leaders.)

Jamie Stewart: While Facebook is good for building a community and your existing network, Twitter is more open. You can use the advanced search for free to find people within a radius of where you are located. You can set up an advanced search of a geographic area and start finding people in that area. You can see what they're saying and start talking to them.

Dayne Gingrich: Twitter has made it simple to connect with like-minded individuals. It has played a huge role in the success of my business. It's been responsible for 75% of my clientele. Twitter allows me to reach a global audience of coaches, players, and successful entrepreneurs -- impossible to reach these same individuals without it. I enjoy engaging and following similar visions and their rise to new levels of success. Twitter makes this all possible. (Dayne is a coach who helps people create a championship mindset for success.)

CHAPTER 19: GETTING STARTED ON TWITTER, PART I

Open an account. Yes, it's really that simple. Go to Twitter.com and follow the easy steps. If you need help, Twitter has help right there.

A step many newbies skip at first is uploading a picture. This is a mistake. Before you tweet or follow more than 20 people, upload a picture. When you fail to post a picture of yourself, an egg shows up. If you start following people, and they see an egg, they will NOT take you seriously.

When uploading a picture, make sure it's a clear, semi-professional picture of yourself. You don't need to be in a suit or business attire, but it should be a really good picture of your face.

Do NOT upload a picture of your logo, your cute pet, your kids, or a quote. People want to connect with YOU, not your logo or your puppy. Make sure your Twitter account is represented by a nice picture of you.

Do not worry about tweeting a lot right away. This will take time. As you grow with Twitter, you'll get your tweeting groove and rhythm down.

It's also easy to get annoyed with the number of tweets from one person, especially when you're new and haven't followed too many people yet. This can be overwhelming or distracting at first, but it will all get worked out in your first month if you follow my trusty steps.

Lastly, write a good bio. How? Easy.

First, review a dozen bios from people who have a lot of followers. Review bios from users who seem like-minded or people that you like. Make sure they are business people, not celebrities. See what you like and what you don't like.

Next, make a quick list of your passions and what you stand for. Add in what you want people to know you for. Keep adding with services or products you provide. This is a chance to put yourself on somewhat of a pedestal. Think highly of yourself when you write your bio. Don't embellish or lie, but do make yourself look like the limitless, powerful human you are.

Once you have reviewed other bios and made your list, just create yours. Perfection doesn't exist, so don't use this step as an excuse to delay building your Twitter empire. You can come back and change your bio anytime I've changed mine several times. It's not permanent.

Follow, get followed

Your first bit of Twitter strategy is to follow people. By following people, you are bound to get followed. Says Bruce Van Horn, "Like network marketing, it's a numbers game. The more people you can put yourself in front of, the more will follow you. I started following 20-30 people a day. I discovered somewhere between 30-50% will follow you back."

Avoid following someone just because you want them to follow you. Follow people you genuinely find interesting, people you know, or people you want to know more about. If they don't follow you back at first, that's okay!

Remember that you can go unfollow anyone at any time, so there's no harm in following someone to see what they're all about. Just do a few seconds of research first.

Before I follow anyone, I take a few seconds to read their bio first. Next, I scroll through a dozen or so of their tweets. I'm looking to make sure they're not pitching like crazy or posting about topics that I have zero interest in. Lastly, I click on their website link and take a look for a few seconds. If all of this makes sense, I follow them.

Later I will get into tools to help you manage your list of followers. It's easy to make yourself feel overwhelmed with your new Twitter adventure, so stop before your head starts spinning.

Trust the process, trust this book, trust me, and be patient. If you want to use Twitter as a productive tool, it will happen in due time. I guarantee it will NEVER happen if you get flustered or give up, so stick with me.....

90 days, 1,000 followers

Getting the most out of Twitter does not mean you need lots and lots of followers. Unless you're a celebrity or a major success already, gaining real followers is going to take time. Remember this when following others. Just because they only have 500 followers doesn't mean they don't have a MASSIVE network connected to them.

One of my closest associates is a speaker who commands a very nice fee to speak for big corporations. He is one of the most influential and connected people I know. However, he only has a few thousand Twitter followers. He decided to focus on quality, not quantity. I tell you this to illustrate that Twitter is about finding the right people, not necessarily finding a lot of people.

All that said, you probably want some followers. There's an easy way to get 1,000 followers or more in your first 90 days on Twitter:

> First, make sure you are tweeting valuable content, retweeting others, thanking people, and commenting on a few posts a day. Don't expect followers if you aren't tweeting daily. A good start is at least five times a day.

> Next, follow at least 20 new people a day. Do this without an agenda, but be discerning. Only follow people who you really find interesting. If you're on the fence about someone, go ahead and follow the person, you can unfollow them at any time.

By doing this, you will be following 100-150 people a week. Many of them are going to follow you back. As a newcomer, this is easily one of the best strategies for growing your followers each day.

Don't follow hundreds of people a day. As you start using Twitter daily, you will run into people who are following 2,001 people. That's because Twitter uses a follower/followee algorithm to keep you from spamming and annoying others (you can view this info in the help area of Twitter).

People who have followed 2,001 have followed too many people without being followed back and have been cut off from following anyone else. Don't fall into this trap. Remember that building your social media and online presence is a marathon, not a sprint. Let's do this the right way – consistently over time.

Techniques for finding good people to follow:

Find someone you follow, and see who follows them. Scan through their followers for bios that catch your eye, again, looking for like-minded people, not people you wish would join your business.

Another great way to get people who actually follow you back is to go through the followers of someone who follows you. Logically, if you follow 10 of their followers, you will get a lot of them following you back.

When someone follows you or you follow them, take a look at who they follow. If it's a like-minded connection, they are probably following people who you would also like to follow.

Search for topics, keywords and hashtags. Remember that hashtags are clickable and they bring up a search for that term. Search for people and words that resonate with you. When I first started on Twitter I looked for coaches, entrepreneurs, speakers, leaders, bloggers, authors, and people in San Diego. I also searched hashtags like #speaking, #marketing, and #SanDiego. Make a quick list of the type of people you want to connect with and use the search feature on Twitter to find people to follow. The search feature at the top of the page is extremely easy to use, so give it a try.

Follow people back! Not everyone, but you're not a celebrity, so don't hold off on following just as many people as follow you. One way to lose good followers is by NOT following people back. You want to be followed, right? So does everyone else.

Another way to lose followers and have people refuse to follow you back is if you blindly follow those who follow you. I'll relay this in a story.

A good friend of mine started on Twitter. He followed my instructions and was doing quite well, tweeting great content and value, making connections, following people. Then one day I decided to look at who he was following. Imagine my shock when I found he was following several dozen adult websites and fake accounts! Why? Not on purpose. He was blindly following anyone who followed him. Mistake.

Look, Twitter is a great thing. With all great things, someone tries to take advantage of it. In social media there are bad people, just like there are bad people in every town. There are pick pockets at Disneyland, but that doesn't make it a bad place to visit. Just because a spammer or adult site follows you, doesn't mean Twitter is an immoral place. Twitter is going to be what you make it. Just be sure to only follow accounts you check out first.

How do you check them out? Good question. Let's review.

Before you follow someone, click on their name or picture and look at their profile. Read their quick bio. Click on the website link they provide. Read a few of their tweets. See what type of people they follow or get followed by. Most of Twitter is clickable, so click around their profile to see if it's to your liking.

This following strategy isn't just mine. I've learned it from experience AND from peers. They are discerning about who they follow back and they also look at someone's followers briefly before they click the follow button. If they see someone is following bad accounts or not paying attention to what they're doing on Twitter, the red flag goes up.

In summary, keep your first 90 days simple. Set up your picture, your bio, and your profile. Tweet several times daily. Respond and thank people. Promote others. Follow 20 people a day. Follow people back (the right people). Do all of this and you will meet some great people, I guarantee it.

Observe and learn

Before you become a tweeting machine, spend a little time observing others. This is a really simple step that can produce compounded results in what you learn and apply.

Start by following people or brands that you like or use. Review what they have tweeted over the last month. Review what gets retweeted. See how people interact with their followers.

As you follow more people, be sure to take time to observe. Look at their profiles. The hashtags they use. The type of pictures they post both in their tweets and on their profile pages. Who do they follow? Who follows them? Take the extra step of looking at their website or blog. The link can be found on their profile page.

Never be afraid to reach out and connect with someone. It's called social media for a reason – it's meant to be social!

Tweet someone when you like what they're up to. Retweet a tweet you find value in. Tell them you like their blog. Promote them to your followers. Contact them through their website to let them know they've impacted you in a positive way.

Humans love feedback, especially positive feedback. Be someone that provides this encouragement, and you will stand out. Genuine compliments are few and far between in today's business world.

One thing to avoid – the use of direct messages on Twitter without connecting first. Direct messages are similar to email or messaging on Facebook. However, this is like spam on Twitter. It will be ignored. Worse, you will be ignored. Only send a direct message after you have mutually followed someone and only after you tweet them first.

Here's how I do it. If I wanted to send you a direct message on Twitter, I would send you a direct message, then immediately tweet you. I would tweet, "Hey, just sent you a DM. It's an interview request. Have a great day!"

You will notice people who will send you a canned direct message when you follow them. This practice doesn't work. Don't do it. This is pitching and spam, not connecting.

A quick note – remember the title of this book. Just because you have promoted someone or met someone like-minded doesn't mean you should pitch them or sell them. Step back! Not everyone is right for your business. There are people you just want to connect with and learn from, and even provide value to without expecting anything in return.

Ask for advice. There is nothing wrong with genuinely asking for someone's advice on your website, your blog, or your online strategy. Once you've made a solid connection with someone, asking for feedback is a great way to tap into their expertise and further establish your relationship. Remember, only ask for feedback if you really want it, and you're going to use it. Do NOT ask for feedback just to prospect someone!

Lastly, any social media channel is going to be what you make it. I once attended a mastermind group that I paid for. It went for three days. I met great people, but there was very little networking and interacting. I left feeling like I wasted my money and time.

Then I realized it was up to me to make the most of it. I connected with a few participants. I started a conference call to get the level of interaction I wanted. I even organized an in-person event in Las Vegas. I made my original investment pay off through hard work and persistence. You can do the same with social media.

APPLICATION:

1. Set up your Twitter account. Make sure you have a good picture and profile. If you already have an account, update your picture and profile info if necessary.
2. Start following 20-25 people a day. Be discerning and do your research.
3. Follow people who follow you back (check them out first).
4. Observe and learn. Take note of what you like and what annoys you. Start engaging.
5. Tweet several times a day and retweet others when you genuinely find value in their content.

CHAPTER 20: GETTING STARTED ON TWITTER – PART II

Will you be in the top 5%?

I've been teaching Twitter courses for a few years now. Because Twitter be can mysterious compared to Facebook, people are very interested. They eagerly attend, listen, and take notes. My courses are very interactive, so there are lots of questions, stories, and practical advice to implement quickly.

Here's what usually happens after my Twitter class:

> 50% of attendees will do nothing. 50% will start a Twitter account or try to get active on a current account. 20% will actually get going on Twitter for at least a week, following my instructions. 10% will stick with it for a month or less. 5% will still be using it after 30 days. Less than 5% will still be active after 90 days.

That's 5 out of 100 people, give or take. I think these stats are typical for anyone interested in a new endeavor. Whether it's writing a book, starting a business, or taking up a hobby. I used to beat myself up thinking it was my teaching, but I was edified when I was asked to do the training almost everywhere I went. I learned that I can give people every piece of training and knowledge I have, but I can't make them do the work.

I don't care what you take up, if you don't do the work and show up, it will NOT work for you. Social media is not an ATM. It's not a lottery ticket.

Be consistent, use it right, follow a strategy, learn and adapt, and you will see results. Disappear and you'll never stand a chance!

So, will you be in the top 5%, or the 95%?

Tweet and retweet

I've already mentioned the importance of tweeting consistently. If you're looking to get noticed, have a voice, and connect with people, you must use that voice. It's essential for momentum. A car gets its best gas mileage on the highway, not stopping and starting in traffic.

Be original

Create your own content. You can do it. Be yourself. Don't try to be a social media expert – you're not. Just be original and be you. The world has enough copy cats. Be the one thing that no one else can be. Be great at it.

Don't fill your stream with too many quotes and retweets. Often I've been retweeted by someone, checked out their bio, and it looked good. Then I reviewed their tweets and couldn't find a single, original tweet or thought. Everything was a retweet or quote. Everything. Don't let that be you. Retweets are great, and essential. Sharing a quote that inspires you is nice. But make those things less than 25% of what you share on all social media sites.

Be sincere

There's great value in promoting someone, retweeting someone, or quoting someone. But make it sincere and genuine. Retweet and share things you really find interesting, valuable, useful, funny, or inspirational. Never retweet someone just because you want their attention or want them to follow or promote you. It just doesn't work that way.

Sure, if you genuinely promote someone, you want that person to follow you. Maybe even deep down you would love it if they reciprocated and retweeted you. That's fine, just don't make it the reason why you're retweeting or promoting.

It reminds me of the guy who tries too hard to get the girl. He tries so hard to be someone she would like that he is no longer himself. If you're constantly trying to be something you're not, you will fail at it.

By being yourself, you will attract the right people. That's what you need in your business AND social media. People will want to connect with you when you're confident in who you are and you show it by adding value whenever you can.

A story about chasing and attraction

When I first started dating my wife, I didn't take it all that seriously. I was flaky. I probably didn't treat her as well as I could. I didn't mistreat her, I just didn't pull out all the stops like I could have. I felt like she was already really interested in me, so I didn't have to work at it. I took her for granted.

Then, she became elusive and disinterested in me. Her attitude was if she wasn't good enough for me, my loss. What? This instantly made me super attracted to her, and I worked hard to win her back.

You see, when you carry yourself with posture and confidence, you become very attractive. By chasing, trying too hard, or not being yourself, you're not having fun, and you're pushing people away. Don't pitch and sell. Not everyone is a candidate for your business. Find the right people by carrying yourself with confidence.

Use your expertise

Everyone is an expert at something. Your experience lends itself to your expertise. It doesn't matter what this expertise is in, you can use it to your advantage.

Social media gives you a chance to leverage this expertise in a powerful way. By articulating it to the world via social networking, in this case Twitter, you're finding like-minded people AND you will attract fans. That's right, fans. To make it big time you need fans. People who look up to you and want some of what you have. They want to work with you and be mentored by you.

Twitter opens you up to an entirely new market and offers a rebirth opportunity. If you are new to Twitter, it's a whole new world, filled with people who want to connect with you.

Use your expertise as part of what you tweet. It doesn't matter if it's gardening, car care, or crafting. Nutrition, fitness, or technology. Leverage that expertise into connections and opportunities. Twitter is a place like no other to do just that.

Content needs a kingdom

If content is king, then connections are the king's castle, army, and kingdom.

Your content is utterly useless without an audience. Your business will never reach its potential without the right connections. So while you are creating a tweeting strategy and magnificent content based on your passion and expertise, remember to network. Connecting with the right person could open you up to a new world of possibilities and prospects. Make time to engage.

Promote others

This has to be one of my favorite things to do on Twitter, and quite possibly the best method I've used to meet great people.

My promotional strategy is very simple: find people and services I like and let my followers know about them. It's just like finding a great restaurant and telling all your friends about it. I love, love, love to help others succeed. I want people (like you) to run down their dreams and capture them. If I can help in a small way by promoting your business, service, blog, website, book, etc., then count on me to do it.

Part of your strategy with EVERY social media channel should be to genuinely promote others with no agenda. Expect nothing in return. Find a love of championing others and you will find great people to connect with.

Lydia Aswolf-Carey's Nine Reasons to Promote Others on Twitter:

1. You or your company look really, really good.
2. Because you look good, your audience immediately broadens.
3. Your reputation/brand strengthens. It's very difficult to be known as a bad guy when you regularly promote other people.
4. When you promote others, some of those others are going to promote you.
5. When you are promoted by others, you gain more followers.
6. Gaining more followers means more engagement.
7. More engagement means potential leads.
8. Promoting potential leads increases your chances of turning them into sales.
9. Sales backed by excellent feedback from those conversions on social media lead to more promotions/followers/leads/conversions.

APPLICATION:

1. Will you be in the top 5%? Take action on this training. Start using Twitter effectively.
2. Find people to promote. Retweet people. Share links to great blogs, articles, or information you find useful.
3. Be original. Go back to your content ideas. Take 15 minutes to brainstorm original tweets you can post.
4. Make time to simply engage. Tell people you appreciate their podcast or a link they shared.

CHAPTER 21: GETTING STARTED ON TWITTER – PART III

Join the conversation

Another way I have grown my network on Twitter is simply by joining the conversation. When someone I follow posts a question that I'm interested in, I reply. When someone replies to one of my tweets, I engage them. Oh, there's that word: **engage**. Follow this philosophy and you can't go wrong – engage and be engaging.

Jamie Stewart sums it up very well: "Social media is not just broadcasting out, it's about the social aspect and connecting with people. There are a lot of distributors just broadcasting their product or opportunity, but they don't engage people. This is the biggest opportunity I see. It's about having a conversation."

Ask questions. Reply to questions. Thank people when they follow or retweet you. Be genuine and have fun.

Use lists

If you've spent any time on your home feed and you are following more than a few people, it can seem overwhelming. Your home feed will only get busier the more people you follow.

Here's how I keep up with key people on Twitter: **lists**.

Lists are easy to create and they make it easy to see a stream of tweets only from users on that list.

For example, I have a list called "Speakers". This list contains 10 people I follow who are professional public speakers. When I want to see what they are tweeting about, I simply click on the list and now I see a feed that only contains my list of speakers.

I can also view the people on that list by clicking on them individually if I want to quickly connect or see only their tweets.

Essentially, lists make it very easy to manage what you see on Twitter so you can customize your experience and make the most of your time. It's like creating your own mini home feed.

Lists have made it very easy for me to retweet the people I like, just by going into that list and seeing all their tweets.

To get help setting up Twitter lists, go to your Twitter account, then go to the Twitter Help Center. Enter "Lists" in the search and you will be given step-by-step instructions.

Hashtags

"What is a hashtag?" and "How do I use hashtags?" are the two most popular questions I get from people who are new to Twitter. I believe that hashtags, because they are so mysterious when you're not familiar with them, can be intimidating. Let's not make them into something they're not!

Hashtags are unique, useful, and a powerful tool on Twitter.

Here is how Twitter itself defines hashtags: *The # symbol, called a hashtag, is used to mark keywords or topics in a Tweet. It was created organically by Twitter users as a way to categorize messages.*

The best way to learn about how to use hashtags and how they work is to experience them. Log in to Twitter, look through your home feed of tweets, and see how people are using hashtags.

Next, click on one. Here's the remarkable feature of hashtags that I've mentioned before – they are clickable and become a search! So when I tweet about #sales, this now becomes a link that can be clicked for more information on that topic.

Hashtags can be something you use regularly for a common term like #wellness, #health, or #leadership, or they can be used as branding. They can also be a way to categorize a special event or topic. For example, many live events will create a hashtag that people can use when tweeting about that event.

Let's say I'm running a big workshop and I tell all the attendees to tweet using the hashtag #StopPitching. As guests tweet with that hashtag, people who are not at the event can tap into this stream and see what's going on.

This type of hashtag works in two great ways: 1) it allows like-minded people to connect surrounding a common theme or event, and 2) it helps market and brand that event.

Companies, conventions, sporting events, organizations, the list goes on and on. They're all tapping into hashtags to help bring people together before, during, and after any kind of event. "People are on social media and television at the same time," explains Jamie Stewart. "Television is seeing this and using it to engage with hashtags during a show."

No need to be in a rush with hashtags or to be worried about using them right off the bat. In fact, it can be better to take your time and learn about them through personal experience. You can't break them, so click on them, check them out, and use them only when you feel comfortable. Plenty of tweets contain no hashtags at all, so take your time with this little phenomenon.

A note about hashtag misuse: Too many hashtags or gibberish hashtags can do more harm than good. By observing hashtag use, you will get a feel for when people are misusing hashtags. Don't be one of those people. When someone sees hashtags being abused, they may unfollow or ignore you.

Repeating your best tweets

Like watching a great movie again or re-reading a book, it's perfectly acceptable to repeat your best tweets. If you get a tweet with a lot of engagement or retweets, use it again. When you should tweet it again depends on your strategy. I like to space them out at least a week, sometimes even a month or two apart.

As you experience Twitter, you will see patterns: when your followers are engaging with your tweets, days of the week and times of the day. If you find you are getting a lot of engagement in the afternoon, you may want to retweet some of your best content during that time. In addition, if your tweet gets great feedback in the afternoon, you may want to try it again in a morning time slot to see what kind of response you get.

I hope you are starting to see that Twitter is something you can only get the most out of by experiencing. It may seem complicated, but all good things that are worth the effort take some time and experience. So stick with it!

Tweetchats

Tweetchats, also called Twitter Chats, are a terrific way to connect with the like-minded. Here's how Forbes Magazine defines them:

A **tweet chat** is a live **Twitter** event, usually moderated and focused around a general topic. To filter all the chatter on **Twitter** into a single conversation, a hashtag is used. A set time is also established so that the moderator, guest, or host is available to engage in the conversation.

If nothing else, Tweetchats are one of the best reasons to become a regular Twitter user.

Tracey Ehman, Honorary Founding Partner of the Women Speakers Association and co-host of the weekly #SpeakerChat on Twitter, explains this further. "Participating in a TweetChat is a great way to make connections with like-minded individuals. It can help you grow your tribe, build awareness, and learn from the experts. TweetChats have not only increased my networking, but also my engagement and influence. Since being a part of #SpeakerChat, I have been contacted for interviews, had requests to be part of telesummits, and been asked to write blog posts."

Here's how they work, as a participant:

Go to TweetChat.com or Twubs.com. There are several other sites that allow you to tap into real-time Tweetchats, but these are the sites I like.

FYI – do NOT use Twitter itself to participate in a Tweetchat. While tempting, it is simply too slow and wonky to actively contribute and keep up.

These sites will ask you to login using your Twitter username and password. Don't worry, this is safe. Once logged in, you simply enter the hashtag you want to follow. Tweetchats include a common hashtag so everyone can follow along and join in. These hashtags are usually unique to the specific chat that day/time, but not always.

Once you have entered the Tweetchat you want to join, it will take you to a page with the chat happening in real-time. There will be a window at the top of the page allowing you to tweet and retweet quickly.

These fast-paced, informative chat sessions are usually moderated by one or two hosts, who will ask a series of questions in an hour or less. These questions will be asked one at a time, allowing about five to six minutes for answers.

You can find a list of Tweetchats by using Google and simply typing in 'list of scheduled Tweetchats'. This will give you days, times, and hashtags of chats taking place throughout the week.

I found out about specific Tweetchats by observing what people were posting and what hashtags they were associating with their posts. I noticed that a lot of people were using #leadfromwithin on a Tuesday evening, so I clicked on that hashtag (remember, hashtags are great because they are links to a search of that key term). This led me to see even more users (people who I don't follow) who were participating in this discussion.

"I know that it can take some time to get used to Twitter and TweetChats, they move very quickly. I would suggest first watching a few chats. See how people ask questions, respond, retweet," advises Tracey Ehman. "Then join in, and don't worry, as you participate in more chats, it will become much easier."

Lolly Daskal describes her #LeadFromWithin Tweetchat, "There are new topics every week and it's grown to 4.5 million people. It's Twitter on Red Bull. For four years it's been bringing thought leaders to other thought leaders. It's about the people who show up."

Lucky for you, I had to learn about Tweetchats the hard way. You get the head start of learning it from my experience. I first tried to participate on Twitter itself and I could not keep up. How did I learn that there was another way to participate? I asked.

Remember, that's one of the GREAT things about the Twitter community. Most people are helpful, friendly, and very responsive.

Some of you have to be thinking at this point, "Yeah, Alex, I joined some chat rooms back in the late 90's or early 2000's. Chat rooms are for geeks, teenagers, and predators." Or maybe you're simply thinking that chats are a time waster that will not produce any results for your business.

Okay, allow me to demonstrate a point. You know the value of an in-person networking event, right? Getting to ask questions, connecting, interacting, and learning. But how can you find like-minded people to connect with and learn from outside of your city or town?

Imagine a networking event where everyone was focused on one topic, contributing to the conversation, sharing knowledge, expertise, and opinions, and helping each other. Sounds pretty good, right? That is a Tweetchat.

Tweetchats are NOT the chat room of 1998, the dating service, or the place to get preyed upon. They are NOT a place to pitch or get pitched on a product or service. They are a safe place FILLED with great minds, thought leaders, and business people. Entrepreneurs, encouragers, and leaders.

There are also Tweetchats for hobbies, causes, and other non-business related topics.

I enjoy Tweetchats because they allow me to find and connect with people I never would have met otherwise. That's pretty much my theme with Twitter. It fills a void in a powerful way. There are people on Twitter just waiting to meet you, connect with you, help you, support you, and inspire you. Practically FREE.

When I participate in a Tweetchat, I usually gain 10-20 incredibly like-minded and valuable followers. To me, that's priceless.

Your business is about meeting and working with the right people. Not just the right people to join your business. No, that's small thinking. Big picture thinking is what we need, my friends! The right people may not join your organization, but they may inspire you to take action. The right person might introduce you to a world of new contacts.

Meeting the right person could mean the advice or idea that sparks a big boost in your income. Connecting with the right leader who believes in you could be the catalyst that propels you to greatness.

"Initially, I participated in Tweetchats to get more followers on my two Twitter accounts," says Michelle Held, who wrote the book *Pinterest Tutorial: Pinterest Help for Beginners*. "What I found was that, with the right Tweetchat, and by that I mean one that suits my interests and professional needs, I learned a lot from like-minded people!"

She continues, "Getting more followers will come naturally when you participate regularly in a Tweetchat that fits you well. These followers will be good quality people who share your interests. Tweetchat followers are valid connections."

"It is imperative that you follow and connect with others on the chats," adds Tracey Ehman. "This is a great opportunity to grow your tribe, connect after the chat, and develop future joint ventures. It is really limitless."

To have a successful network marketing business that makes all your wildest dreams come true requires more than people buying from you. It takes meeting the right people, giving value, and leveraging relationships in a powerful way. Tweetchats can be a small piece of your networking strategy that leads to bigger, long-term results.

The key that starts your car is small, especially compared to the size and power of your vehicle. Yet that little piece is the catalyst to igniting something with incredible force. In the same way, participating in Tweetchats could be a difference maker for you.

Remember the marathon approach! Joining one Tweetchat and expecting sales or huge results is foolish and frankly, stupid. Plan on participating in at least two Tweetchats a month. Try a couple different subjects to meet diverse people and find out what floats your boat. Make them part of your social media strategy for the next year. Yes, the next year. You're in this for the long haul, remember?

Give Tweetchats a try. You might even find me on one of them!

Anyone can host a Tweetchat, but that doesn't mean you should. At least not yet. My recommendation for just about everyone reading this book is to hold off on hosting a Tweetchat. Instead, learn the ropes, get a following, connect with people, and enjoy the ride.

APPLICATION:

1. Create your first Twitter list. This is a group of people you follow. If you click on the same button where you log out, you will see "Lists." If you need help, visit the help center on Twitter.
2. Start using hashtags, when appropriate. If you're not comfortable using them yet, take some time to observe how they're being used.
3. Participate in your first Tweetchat. #LeadFromWithin is a good one. Find a chat that looks interesting and join the conversation without pitching or selling.

CHAPTER 22: TWITTER TOOLS

When building anything, you need the proper tools. Social media is no different, especially Twitter. There are a plethora of tools available, each with its own pros/cons and individual fit. The key is to find which tool(s) you enjoy using.

Once I find a tool I like that gets the job done, I tend to stick with it. To find what works best for you, try a few out. Think of it like trying on a pair of running shoes. I can recommend what I use, of course, but you will only find out what works best for you by trying it on for size.

This book is based on my experience and the experiences and expertise of my close, professional network. So in this chapter I will NOT recommend any tools I haven't used, but I do encourage you to Google what's out there and ASK for help from people using social media effectively.

Hootsuite

Almost everyone I know who does social media for a living or relies on it as part of their marketing and networking funnel uses Hootsuite. What is Hootsuite? Here's how Wikipedia describes it:

Hootsuite is a social media management system for brand management. The system's user interface takes the form of a dashboard, and supports social network integrations for Twitter, Facebook, LinkedIn, Google+, Foursquare, MySpace, WordPress, TrendSpottr and Mixi.

I love that term, dashboard. Hootsuite provides an in depth display of your social media channels, stats, communication, and scheduling.

There is a free version and paid version of Hootsuite. I use the free version, it suits my needs. Check out the free version first until you get the hang of it. Once you understand it, use it, and like it, then you can consider the paid options.

I use Hootsuite exclusively for Twitter. However, my wife uses Hootsuite for both Twitter and Facebook. From Wikipedia's description, you can see that it can be integrated with many of the major social media channels.

I use Hootsuite primarily to manage and schedule future tweets on Twitter. You can use it in this fashion for the other social media sites listed as well, including Facebook. Being able to post while you're offline, doing something else, or at strategic times are some of the benefits for me.

For example, if you are hosting an event in your town and want to tweet once a day on Twitter, you could schedule the tweets for different days and times. So while you're driving to an appointment, that strategic Twitter post will magically go up without you having to be online to do so.

Hootsuite allows me to keep a steady stream of tweets rolling every day, while also viewing what I have scheduled in the future. This allows me to view my strategy on one dashboard.

Of course, I still tweet live and in person, but scheduled tweets make up about 50% of my tweeting on any given day.

Hootsuite's greatest benefit to me: time management.

As an entrepreneur, your time is worth more than gold. It's very easy to get lost and spend countless hours on social media. This is not productive. This is why it's ultra-important to take a strategic, thoughtful approach to your platform.

Hootsuite allows me to maximize my time, spending quality time doing what I want to do – connect and network instead of strategize and plan. I take about 20 minutes every Sunday evening to plan out my week of tweets using Hootsuite. This lets me spend the week replying to retweets, retweeting others, joining the conversation, participating in Tweetchats, and connecting.

JustUnFollow

JustUnFollow.com is a site that you can utilize to track people who follow you, people who unfollow you, inactive followers, fans, etc. It provides a quick and easy page for you to manage your followers and who you follow.

Why is this important? Great question. Managing your followers on Twitter itself can be a bit overwhelming, I've found. Think of it like going to a specialist. Sure, your primary care doctor can look at your foot, but if you need foot surgery you're going to see a podiatrist. While Twitter is great, tools like JustUnFollow.com hone in on specialized areas, making it easier to get the results you're looking for.

I use JustUnFollow to:

Review people who have followed me who I have not followed back. I can then decide if I'm going to follow them back. I like this feature because I see people who I do want to follow but I've missed for some reason.

See who unfollowed me. I'm not a tit for tat sort of person, and I don't recommend you be that way on social media either. However, there are people who will follow you, wait until you follow them back, then a few days later they will unfollow you. It's a game a few people play to make it look like they have a ton of followers without following a lot of people, sort of like a celebrity. I would never know unless I looked through everyone I followed to see if they are following me back. With JustUnFollow, I see these types of people right away.

You will see people occasionally unfollow you who you may think you've developed a connection with. It's okay. It's rarely personal and if it is, so what. Stick to your game and keep your head up. You will find the right people to connect with!

I view inactive people I follow. I can pull lists of people who I follow that haven't been active on Twitter in over one month, three months, or six months or more. I unfollow people if they are not going to be actively consistent on Twitter. I usually put the threshold at three months of inactivity.

Twimemachine

Twimemachine.com allows me to view a history of my past tweets. I use it to see who has retweeted me in the past, who I've retweeted or connected with, and old tweets that I may want to tweet again.

Like a diary, it's nice to be able to spend a few minutes looking over your tweeting history so you can make adjustments to your strategy.

More tools

New tools are being created all the time to help you navigate the world of social media successfully.

Take time to do a Google search on social media tools so that you can find something that will work for you.

APPLICATION:

1. Visit Hootsuite.com to set up your account. Their basic account is free. Click around and get familiar with the features.
2. Schedule a few tweets in the future. Get comfortable using their scheduler.
3. If you need assistance, visit the help area of Hootsuite for any technical questions you have or any instructions you need.
4. Another tool people use with Twitter is Tweetdeck. I have not used this tool, but I have heard good things about it.
5. When you're ready, check out other social media tools available to you, like JustUnFollow and Twimemachine.

SECTION 6: ADDITIONAL CHANNELS

Speaker Stephen Shapiro tells a great story through his blog about marketing his speaking business.

Over the years he's tried hiring marketing and public relations firms to implement direct marketing programs, improve his search engine optimization (SEO), and secure key spots in newspapers, magazines and television. He's also paid for online advertising campaigns. All of this to expand his network, increase traffic to his website, and raise awareness of his brand and services.

After all of this work and expense, he stopped and did a self-analysis of where his business had been generated. With the exception of one paid speech, all of his paid speeches over the last 18 months were generated from existing or previous relationships. The work came from past clients, audience members, and referrals.

I love the way Stephen words his conclusion to his findings: nurture your network.

Depending on what statistics you read, the probability of getting a sale from an existing customer is 50-75%. The chance of landing a new prospect is somewhere between 1-20%, and it often costs a lot more in marketing dollars and time to secure new business in the cold market.

My friends, social media not only makes it easier than ever to expand your warm market, it also provides an exceptional opportunity to nurture your current network. By caring for your network and connecting, you put yourself in a position for people to think of you when they're looking for a solution.

This is the power of the Stop Pitching, Start Connecting strategy. It focuses on nurturing your network. Taking care of people who take care of you. Empowering and promoting others with no agenda and zero expectations.

Of course, I want you to use social networking to meet new people. I want your network to grow like never before. I want you to have new opportunities and new relationships. But as we talk about additional social media channels, I also want you to think about nurturing your current database of contacts. Think about using social media to strengthen and grow already existing relationships. Reconnect with people. Increase your referability.

Behind every person you know could be thousands of people who are looking for what you have to offer.

CHAPTER 23: FACEBOOK

"It's kind of cool to post something on Facebook and get a bunch of people to talk about it" –JB Glossinger

Facebook, by far, is the most popular social media channel. Most likely, many of your Facebook friends are people you already know.

Facebook and Twitter are totally different animals, but both have great uses for connecting, which is why I advocate using both.

Facebook is an exceptional communication tool for your current network. I like it because it can be used as a gathering place for your team or organization. You can also create groups that allow people to connect and share. It's a great place to post news, updates, and specials.

"We're in the business of conversations. I think that anytime you can stay in touch and communicate and network, it's good," says BK Boreyko.

While it isn't as easy to find new people to connect with as some other social media sites, Facebook is really good for making deeper connections, building trust, and growing your referability. It's also a place to test and grow your subtle, or passive marketing approach. There seems to be a deeper emotional connection on Facebook versus other sites.

Because most of your Facebook friends already have some level of trust in you, that barrier has already been broken. You can organically reach more people through their network. If the average Facebook user has 100 friends, that's a potential for 10,000 or more referrals. (The number of average Facebook friends varies by source.)

However, because this trust is already built, it can be easy to chase people away if you start pitching. I've seen this happen over and over. Someone sees one other person with an offer on Facebook, and they turn into a used car salesperson. Every day they post about joining their team, buying their products, or something about their company. This type of strategy will get you a tiny bit of sales, but largely ignored or worse, unfriended.

Facebook fits perfectly into the **Stop Pitching** strategy. Think about these stats from the Pew Research Center on why women and men are using Facebook:

- Seeing photos or videos: women 54%, men 39%
- Sharing with many people at once: women 50%, men 42%
- Seeing entertaining or funny posts: women 43%, men 35%
- Learning about ways to help others: women 35%, men 25%
- Receiving support from people in your network: women 29%, men 16%

Nobody logs in to Facebook or friends someone to get pitched or sold, but they do want to be entertained. They want support. They want to see photos. They want to be inspired. And they want to share with a lot of people.

BOOM!

This means if you continue to earn their trust, provide valuable content, and take the connecting approach instead of the pitching approach, your Facebook friends can turn into customers, business partners, or refer you. Not all of them, mind you. In fact, not most of them. But some of them. Most importantly, the right people.

This is a good time to remind you about **subtle marketing**. Take a more passive approach. Build connections and trust. By doing so, you will get more chances to present what you have to offer. "I treat everybody with respect. It doesn't take a lot of time. I budget my time and get on Facebook once or twice a day. I want people to know that I care – because I really do," explains Chris Freytag. "I'm proud of people who make changes or get healthy. It's all about **connecting** and how much you care. People don't care how much you know until they know you care. This is an emotional business, you have to show it and have it."

While Facebook is primarily about relational connection, that doesn't mean you can't post things that relate directly to your business. Mitzi Dulan, uses it strategically to give people helpful content that supports her business. "I use Facebook to share recipes and tips. I also post my television appearances and news articles that I have been quoted in from NYDailyNews.com, Yahoo.com, FoodNetwork.com, etc. People also love to know some personal information, like what my family eats. I have learned that posts about my kids are very popular. I love sharing great articles that I find and inspirational quotes."

One other note: according to a Pew Research Center study, only 10% of Facebook users update their status daily. However, 44% of users 'like' content posted by their friends on a daily basis.

Ways to use Facebook effectively:

1. **Get the basics right**

   If you want people to view you as a businessperson, make sure your profile picture is a good photo of *you*. Not your pet, not your products, not a logo. People don't want to connect with a logo unless you're Nike or Apple. Make sure your photo is recognizable and fairly consistent with other profile pictures you use on social media and the web.

   Also, use a relevant cover image on your personal page. This is the picture or banner at the top of the page. It should give a glimpse of who you are, what you stand for, or something powerful or inspirational. Again, this should NOT be your company, your products, or a slogan about your opportunity. People are friends with *you*.

   Be positive at all times and know that everything you post is a reflection of your personal brand. "Perspective people who could hire you [or work with you] are checking out your Facebook page," says Chris Freytag. "I separate my personal page from my business page. My personal account is only for my family. On my business page I uphold standards and morals I believe in. I am who my brand is."

Great advice.

2. Post great content

Remember the 90/10 rule. It's important to provide a good mix of content between entertainment, education, and personal posts. When you do decide to post something about your business or product, avoid the hard sell. Be subtle, passive, and fun about it instead.

People love visuals on Facebook. Pictures, videos, and infographics are all eye catching. Remember that everything you do online is a reflection of your personal brand, so be mindful of what you post.

A one-track mind won't be very engaging to your Facebook friends, so be diverse with your posts as well. Be yourself, but vary your posts.

3. Know your friends

Gauge how your friends respond to your posts and the posts of others. Take notice of when your friends are active, both days and times. Watch what other people post – what you like and what you don't like. Never post divisive comments or engage in an unfriendly debate on Facebook.

Quick story about a networker who sent her friends running for the hills. We'll call her Barb (not her real name).

Barb got involved with an internet marketing company. They were essentially marketing blog and web space. She was excited about it and started posting about it on Facebook, pitching the opportunity. Suddenly, 80-90% of her posts were about this new company.

Her friends on Facebook wanted the old Barb back. They missed the updates on her kids and personal life. They wanted to see travel and vacation pictures. Instead, they were bombarded with invites to events and non-stop selling.

It got so bad that one of her friends said to me, "We're all unfriending Barb. We just can't take it. She can't draw the line. She posts about XYZ company on all of our pages. Every day! It's really sad."

Don't be like Barb. Know your friends. Be a friend. Stop pitching and start connecting.

4. **Craft a great posting strategy**

This requires some testing and experimenting on your part. Test the length of your posts, the type of posts, when you post, and how often you post.

What gets the most engagement? When and what are people sharing? When you find something that people like and/or share, craft more content like it. Start slowly. You can always ramp up the frequency of your posts as you go, but if you post too often you may lose friends or be ignored.

Remember to include visual content often, like pictures, to create engagement with people who like that. Photo collages, albums, graphics, and links are all visually appealing.

Find a balance between personal, value-based, and business content to post.

5. Engage

This is perhaps the most critical piece – engaging and connecting. Take time every day to genuinely like and comment on posts. Share when appropriate. Promote great people and businesses you use. Praise people who accomplish something or do something good. Be yourself and turn off that urge to sell, sell, sell. Instead, just be human and enjoy your Facebook friends.

Facebook has a confidential algorithm they use to determine what shows up in your news feed. While they've been covert about how this works, they have confirmed that engaging, connecting, liking, commenting, and sharing will influence what you see. On the flipside, the more people comment, like, and share what you post, the more likely your posts are to show up in the news feed of your friends on Facebook. Remember, never like, comment, or share with any agenda other than genuinely connecting. When you're genuine, reciprocation happens in magical ways. When you force it, you push people away. We've all had those people in our lives we hate to ask for favors because they expect something in return. Don't be one of those people on social media!

6. Practice subtle marketing

So you're ready to let some of your Facebook friends know what products you have to offer and how they can get them. Here are a few quick suggestions to do this in a more subtle, passive way:

Put your products in the light of everyday life. If they revolve around weight loss or fitness, post before/after pictures with links on how to order. Include lifestyle images and stories of

146

what people have accomplished on these products. The mom who can now run a half marathon. The dad who can take his shirt off at the beach without feeling self-conscious. The 20-something who has a blossoming social life because her confidence has returned.

Lifestyle images and stories get attention. The ability to get a new car. Taking time off on your own terms. Traveling on that dream vacation. The mountain getaway with the family. This type of passive marketing makes people want to ask you how you're making all this happen.

Share pictures of recognition and events. Many people stay in network marketing for the comradery. They want to belong to something. In addition, most people don't receive any recognition at their jobs or in their personal lives. By sharing the good things happening in your business, you can **create curiosity**.

7. Events

Facebook's event feature allows you to invite people and promote your upcoming event. This is an exciting tool that can help you if used properly and not abused. Don't overuse this feature – be strategic.

Choose the right people to invite to your events. Like emails, when you 'spam' people it tends to get ignored. If you invite too often or blindly, people will tune out your invites. If it's an in-person event, don't invite people in other states who have no way to attend. That's spam. Also, before you invite a new acquaintance, think about how you would feel about getting invited to their event. If it feels awkward or weird, take note and hold off on inviting them to your event.

If there is someone who you feel could truly benefit from your event, send them a message or post to their wall. Just remember the 90/10 rule. Also, ask invitees who have confirmed their attendance to talk up the event to other invitees who haven't responded yet.

Make sure you engage with your own event. Post on the event wall. Send an update. If there's news or excitement, share it.

All kinds of events can be shared on Facebook, not just parties or in-person events. You can create a virtual event via conference call or webinar to attract people from any geographic location.

8. **Promoting/boosting posts**

Here's a little trick that can work very effectively when used properly. When you're ready to promote a big webinar, event, or infoproduct, consider boosting or promoting that post on Facebook. You can find step by step instructions for doing this in the help section of Facebook itself. Boosting your post will cost very little (usually $5-$15), but it can dramatically increase your reach.

This is not something you want to do every day or even every week, but it will be something you should experiment with if you're serious about using Facebook in your business.

Boosting or promoting a post will allow you, in some cases, to reach friends of friends of friends. That's right – it can expand who sees your post by thousands of people. It's important to test your strategy and have something really good to promote when you boost a post so you can maximize results.

Your personal profile vs. a business/fan page on Facebook

Your personal page is officially called your Profile. Facebook also offers a business page that is called a Page, and it is designated for brands and businesses. When people want to be part of your personal profile, they friend request you and you have to approve. Anyone can like your business page and therefore see the posts.

Your personal profile is designed for being social with friends, family, and acquaintances. A business page is for promoting, communicating, and sharing aspects of a business or brand. Remember that you are your best brand, so having a business page is something to consider.

Facebook has recently added a feature called 'follow' that you can add to your personal profile. This allows people to see your public posts/news feed without having to be your friend. The benefit for you is that you can have people interested in you see what you're up to, but keep your friends limited and segregate what you post. This is a great option in lieu of or in addition to having a business page.

The big question most entrepreneurs and Facebook users have is, "How can I get my posts to show up more often on other people's news feeds?" As I mentioned earlier, there is a bit of a mystery shrouding this. Facebook does not reveal the algorithm they use to determine what posts show up on your news feed, higher on your news feed, or not at all. The same principle applies to a business page as it does to your personal page: Connect. Surprised? The more connecting you do, the more likes, comments, and shares you will get, therefore increasing your chances of showing up on news feeds.

My recommendation is to start by developing your personal brand through your personal profile. Add the follow option to your profile if you wish. Once you feel good about your strategy, voice, and brand, consider creating a business page. Don't start a Facebook business page just because you're trying to keep up with someone else or you think you have to do it. Take it slow. Many times it's best to let things organically happen when it feels right or gains momentum.

Until then, check out business pages. Ask a few other Facebook users who are also entrepreneurs or like-minded if they have a business page. Take a look at how people are using their personal profiles to connect and occasionally promote or create curiosity.

Lastly, if you decide to start a business page on Facebook, invite everyone you know to check it out. There's nothing wrong with promoting the page. In fact, it's a smart thing to do. Just make sure your business page offers value to people and gives them a reason to like it (which is NOT sales).

Facebook groups

This feature allows you to create a private page for a select group of people. For example, you could set up a Facebook group page for your organization or a group of people on your team. Following the connecting strategy, you could also set up a group for the parents of your child's soccer team, for your meetup group, or for the local entrepreneur group.

A private group can be created for just about anybody, and allows only those group members to see and comment on the posts. It provides a great space to share and communicate while having control over who's in the club.

Facebook currently allows three types of groups: secret, closed, and open. As the titles say, the secret group is only known and seen by the group members; the closed group is only open to group members but outsiders can see who is in the group (but not the posts); and open, or public groups allow anyone to see the group, the group members, and posts.

Facebook groups are easy to create and can be a safe place for your team to talk shop without outside influence. "The Facebook group feature works really well for managing and providing support and discussion for a particular business, topic, or association," states Tracey Ehman.

I use Facebook daily to keep in touch with my current network and add people that I meet elsewhere. If I meet someone through a business contact, networking, my hockey league, etc., there's a good chance I will expand the relationship to Facebook. It's also been a great tool to reconnect with friends and associates I've lost contact with.

As you connect on Facebook keep in mind that you are using it as a business tool. Some people hop on Facebook to network and an hour later they realize they are still lost in this world. I spend about 10 minutes a day on Facebook, 15 minutes on a heavier day. I use it every day to stay on top of my personal network, with a little business mixed in. Set a timer if Facebook is a timewaster temptation during your work hours. There's nothing wrong with using social media to play or wind down after a hard day's work. Just be sure it doesn't hurt your productivity.

APPLICATION:

1. How can you be more engaging on Facebook? Think about posting more images, links, and visual elements.
2. Spend time each day commenting on and liking posts.
3. Do you have the basics right? Start with your photo and profile page.
4. Gauge your posting strategy. Be mindful of the day of the week, time of day, and frequency of posts. What's getting a lot of engagement and likes?
5. Start posting your offer in a more subtle, or passive way. Brainstorm ways you can create curiosity instead of pitching.

CHAPTER 24: INSTAGRAM

"I can make one post on Instagram and it goes to the other sites. A picture is worth a thousand words. It's imagery and it's fast." –BK Boreyko

Instagram is a mobile photo and video sharing social network. This channel allows for sharing pictures on multiple other networks, including Facebook (who, as I mentioned earlier, owns Instagram). One of its most liked features is the ability to filter photos and add effects, making your mobile shots look cool, professional, unique, or fun.

Because of how Instagram works, posting pictures from a mobile device, it is NOT a good tool for pitching, whatsoever. Trying to sell on Instagram will get you ignored, guaranteed.

It *is* a fantastic social network for subtle marketing, especially if you love taking pictures with your phone. If you don't like taking pictures, Instagram is NOT for you.

Two of the useful things about Instagram are the ability to tag others in photos and the use of hashtags, much like Twitter. It creates an even playing field when done correctly and not abused.

For example, a popular local restaurant may not follow you back on Twitter, but they are very likely to follow you back on Instagram if you post a great picture promoting them. It's one of the nuances unique to Instagram, and a reason why being on multiple social networks can be a good thing.

A word of caution: do not join Instagram just because you feel like you have to. Because it is photo-centric, it's more of a fun way to connect, but you should still employ a strategy. If it feels complicated or that it could be too much on top of what you're already doing or learning, it probably is.

If you check out Instagram and you like it, you may find it works well with your Facebook or other social media account. If you love taking pictures and sharing them, and you can do it in a fun and strategic way, Instagram could be for you.

A few recommendations for Instagram:

- Follow people. If you want to be followed, you've got to be a follower on Instagram.
- Like pictures you really like. If you want people to like your pictures, engage with other users.
- Take good pictures. Blurry pics, offensive pics, or pics that are too personal won't help you and could hurt your personal brand.
- Too many cutesy pics (kittens, babies, etc.) or too many selfies won't perpetuate your personal brand as a businessperson or entrepreneur.
- Be strategic with your photos. This is where the 90/10 rule comes into play. Instagram can help you connect with people about your offer if you don't bombard followers with it. Incorporate your products or opportunity into lifestyle pictures. Instagram offers a chance to have a little fun and not have to create great content, but simply photograph life. Build your opportunity or products into what you do to create curiosity. Subtle marketing!
- Be careful not to inundate your followers with too many posts. Instagram is a place for quality, not necessarily quantity.
- Observe and learn like any other social network. If you're really interested in learning how to use Instagram effectively, jump in, and spend time watching how others do it.
- When you promote a company, restaurant, etc., it allows you to connect with people who are also fans of those businesses. So, if you eat a great meal somewhere, post a picture of your main dish, tag the restaurant and use a relevant hashtag. Other people who like it will follow you. BOOM!

- Get trained. Sites like Mashable and YouTube offer free training and tutorials on Instagram so you can learn the basics. Just go to Google or YouTube and search for the specific training you need.
- Instagram should NOT be your primary channel for connecting through social media. It can play a significant role, but deeper connections will happen through Facebook, Twitter, or LinkedIn. Consider using Instagram to make connections that move to one or more of these other sites.

"When I think of Instagram, I think of it to instigate," explains Chris Freytag. "I start from there, then link to Twitter and Facebook, and continue to build from there. I use Instagram because it fits my personality and who I am. I post what happens to me during the day, motivation, and variety."

Instagram should be a fun addition to your social media toolbox. It's not a place to prospect or sell, but it can be a place to create new connections.

APPLICATION:

1. Do you really like taking pictures with your phone? If so, Instagram may be for you. If not, try another network.
2. You can join Instagram for free and start following. Download the app on your smartphone. Observe and learn.
3. Ask your friends and family if they're on Instagram. If so, follow them.
4. If you're already using Instagram, check your strategy. If you're posting too many product pictures, adapt your style. If you're not using hashtags, learn how. Have fun!

CHAPTER 25: LINKEDIN

LinkedIn is a social media channel specifically for business networking. The site allows you to connect to people via invites. People you connect with on LinkedIn are called "Connections." Can you see why I like LinkedIn?

LinkedIn uses a gated approach to connections – meaning you need to know the person you are attempting to connect with. When you invite or ask someone to connect, you then specify how you know that person. If the invitee claims they don't know you or that your attempt is spam, your account will be flagged. Too many of these types of responses could result in your account being restricted or closed. So, when using LinkedIn, be genuine with your connections.

LinkedIn is great for connecting with people you may have forgotten about or have worked with in the past. It allows you to see connections of connections. This means every time you obtain a new connection on LinkedIn, you can view their connections and invite people to connect with you.

I must take a minute to remind you that if you try to sell on LinkedIn, you will be ignored, or worse. If you use it to pitch, you're missing the point. This social network is for professionals. It's an awesome tool to network with business people and get referrals. Active selling will not work on LinkedIn unless you build **trust**.

LinkedIn is also its own animal, so people you connect with here may not be your Facebook friends or followers on Twitter. Similar to other sites I've used, LinkedIn has allowed me to connect with hundreds of people that otherwise I would have lost touch with. Former co-workers from years past. Associates and networkers I've worked with and known well. Executives and leaders from companies I've been with or that I've met over the years. Vendors I have done business with.

The messaging feature on LinkedIn allows you to communicate with people, even if you don't have their email address or phone number.

LinkedIn is not a social site where you're posting your daily activities or quick posts about life. Consider it more like a living contact database of your professional network. As it has grown, LinkedIn incorporated some great tools that allow you to showcase your work, post blogs, and join specified groups.

What I like about LinkedIn is the ability to connect, message, and endorse people that I may not be close friends with, but have a good working history with. Any tool that allows me to find people who I never thought I would see or hear from again is something worth utilizing. The endorsement feature is a nice layer too. I can endorse you for a specific topic/skill from a list, or I can write a recommendation or endorsement on your profile.

I recommend checking LinkedIn once a day for a few minutes and signing up for their alerts. Whenever someone sends me an invite or when people are checking out my profile, I am alerted via email. That's when I go in and check LinkedIn, reply to invites, view connections, and make a few invites of my own.

If you're not already on LinkedIn, getting an account is free. Here are some basic tips for getting started:

- Create a good profile. Keep it truthful and genuine and include your relevant work history and education.
- Include pertinent skills or accomplishments, including volunteer experience.
- Write a summary that's brief, concise, and focused on your relevant skills.
- Post a clear, professional picture of yourself. Not a product or a brand. A photo of you.
- Your LinkedIn profile is not strictly a resume. Feel free to be a little more personable on this page.

- Start connecting. LinkedIn will walk you through setup, so don't fret. You can allow LinkedIn to access your contacts and it features a "People You May Know" page to help you. Start by getting at least 50 connections. Have fun with it.
- Send a few messages to your new connections. Ask them what they've been up to. Ask them how they like LinkedIn. Thank them for connecting with you.
- If you're already on LinkedIn, make sure your profile and picture are updated. Expand your connections.

LinkedIn, like most other social networks, takes time to learn, understand, and use well. You have to experience it. Play with it. Click around. Ask people what they like about it. Read a few articles and tips about it. See how it fits into your arsenal of social media sites and tools.

I highly recommend getting on LinkedIn if you're not already. It fits the **Stop Pitching and Start Connecting** model to grow your warm market, including *reconnecting*.

APPLICATION:

1. Use the steps listed in this chapter to start using LinkedIn – it's free.
2. If you're already using LinkedIn, check out all the features and tools. Connect and reconnect with people today.
3. Ask a few of your connections what they like about LinkedIn and how they use it.

CHAPTER 26: PINTEREST

"Pinterest was the first time I met someone on a social network and then met them in person. I started chatting, trading pins, had coffee together, and ended up doing business with them." –Michelle Held, author of *Pinterest Tutorial: Pinterest Help for Beginners.*

Pinterest describes itself as a visual discovery tool. Visuals, called "Pins" are placed on "Boards" – you can think of it like pinning something to a bulletin board that you can share with other Pinterest users. Pinterest has a tool that you can install on your web browser that allows you to pin things from other sites with one click of a button.

Mitzi Dulan found a perfect fit with her market there. "I absolutely LOVE Pinterest!" she said. "Recipes pins are extremely popular on Pinterest. Workout plans, exercise ideas, and inspirational quotes are also very popular. It allows me to influence and share all of my favorite nutrition and fitness information. It is also a huge traffic driver to my website and to the websites that I pin to."

She continues, "I recommend people pin about 80% educational and inspirational and about 20% promotion. You can create Pinterest boards for so many different areas of interest, and research has shown that Pinterest drives purchases."

Pinterest demographics will vary by source, but most will agree that it's dominated by women (80-90% of users) and the majority of users are over age 35.

Seem like a fit for network marketing? If you said yes, I wholeheartedly agree with you. If you are representing products that are visually appealing or lend themselves well to recipes (as Mitzi Dulan states, recipes are very popular on Pinterest), and appeal to women, this social networking site might fit you and your business like a glove.

When it comes to learning how to use Pinterest, I recommend that you learn by doing. Experience it by joining and observing. Steve Gutzler agrees, "With Pinterest, I looked at the top Pinterest guy, did boards similar to him, learned from him, and now I have a presence."

Similar to other sites like Instagram, keywords play a big role in what you pin because people can search for them. You can also tag other users in a pin. Categories also play a pivotal role in getting noticed on Pinterest. "If you don't choose a category for a board, you will never show up in a search for that category," explains Michelle Held.

Mitzi Dulan adds, "I am always learning what is most effective and looking at the most recent research on Pinterest for the most popular words. I have also gained a lot of information from my own pins of what types of pins seem to be the most successful for getting pinned and repinned."

Here are some of Michelle Held's top tips for Pinterest:

- Do the simple things right: a good profile, good descriptions, and give your boards a category.
- Add boards, lots of boards. Anything that can sideways relate to what you do (think subtle marketing).
- It can't be all about what you're selling. Can't be 'my product, my product, my product'. It's boring and it's not interacting with the community.
- Join group boards. Pin to them. Pin back to those boards. Pin back to other users. You want to pin both ways. Those people get a notification that you've pinned to their board. It's the same concept as tweeting and retweeting on Twitter. It's estimated that 80% of pins are re-pins.
- If you have a blog or website, make sure it has images and photographs that can be pinned. Create graphics that are re-pinable. You can take a graphic or quote and watermark it with your website.
- You have to appeal to the majority, which is women. Women are spending money and Pinterest users are educated.

- Drive traffic to the outlets you are on. The combination of a blog, Pinterest-specific graphics, with a LinkedIn profile can drive traffic.
- Interact with the community.
- Give it some time – I'm talking in the six month range. 400 followers seems to be the magic number. Give it a chance to work for you.

APPLICATION:

1. Is Pinterest for you? It's a very visual platform. Join for free and check it out.
2. If you're already on Pinterest, follow Michelle's simple tips to ramp up your engagement and connections.
3. Check out Michelle Held's book: *Pinterest Tutorial: Pinterest Help for Beginners* on Amazon.

CHAPTER 27: YOUTUBE

I've seen quite a few people who have started YouTube channels, only to do more harm than good to their business or personal BRAND. Posting zany videos of yourself wearing a costume, drunk exploits, or long-winded talking head pieces probably won't help expand your network with your ideal clients or prospects.

I've also seen it used as a time waster. Spending six weeks trying to make the perfect viral video then quitting YouTube will do you absolutely no good. In fact, while viral videos can help you a lot, most people who create them will tell you **consistency** is the key.

Luck takes discipline. You've probably heard the legend that it took Thomas Edison a thousand tries before inventing the light bulb. Yet, according to Edison, it simply took him a thousand steps to create a successful invention. Only the truly dedicated and persistent make their dreams come true.

Jared McMullin, a YouTuber who runs a show called *Friday Night Cranks* has videos with over 12 million views. He shared something that surprised me at the time. He said most of his videos that get millions of view are well over a year old. In fact, most of them were recorded and posted three to five years ago. So his 'viral' videos aren't some case of wacky luck or overnight success. They are a product of him posting videos every single week for years and years.

Consistency, my friends. A long-term, marathon approach. These are the so-called 'secret' ingredients to online fame. It's not the smartest, savviest, luckiest, or most talented people who rise to the top. Sure, those things help. But above all it's the simple, little things done over and over that make people successful in any endeavor, and YouTube (and social media and network marketing for that matter) is no different.

I view YouTube as one of the greatest 'how to' resources in the world (hint, hint – want people to view your YouTube videos? Post some 'how to's'). Whatever concept you have, make at least one instructional video packed with value. I restrung a pull starter on a generator thanks to YouTube. Really. There's no way I could have done this on my own, without someone showing me what to do.

I'm a visual learner mixed with kinesthetic, or hands-on learning. Meaning, I have to see it done and then do it myself. Audio and written instructions do very little for me. I prefer to watch it being done first. YouTube works great for this. I've installed the electrical for a trailer hitch, learned to brew beer, and helped with my kids' school projects all thanks to YouTube.

Bruce Van Horn suggests, "There are people who love to watch stuff. Those people love YouTube. It's the second largest search engine in the world. If someone has a question, if they don't know how to do something, they go onto YouTube."

YouTube is a good place to park or house relevant videos you create. It's a visual outlet where you can send people to see more about you and what you offer. You can post videos from YouTube on your website and share them on most other social networks.

YouTube is owned by Google, so one advantage is that your videos can show up easier in a Google search. On the flipside, if you make lame videos, people can see them very easily and get turned off before ever meeting you.

Some YouTube basics from Jared McMullin:

- Post as consistently as possible. Try and post at the same time every week. If you are consistent, videos will be there for your subscribers.
- If you don't post videos, people aren't going to show up.
- YouTube is quality over quantity.

- It's called YouTube, it's about you. Don't change your videos or who you are just to appease people. Be yourself.

What equipment do you need?

Let's start with your camera. With the quality of today's smartphones, you can take video and upload it directly to YouTube. This is great for spur of the moment content, lifestyle videos, or if you're just getting started. However, your first upgrade should be a camera that shoots in 1080p high definition. Most of today's higher end digital cameras also shoot outstanding video.

No one wants to view shaky videos, so make sure you use a tripod. These can be found inexpensively. It will free up hands and help produce stable video.

Next, think about upgrading your sound quality. Most phones and video cameras do not capture good, crisp, sound. There are a few easy ways to remedy this. You could get a microphone that plugs into your camera. These can be hand-held or clip to your clothing. You could also purchase a separate audio recorder and match it up to your video. Good recording microphones are not terribly expensive ($89-$400) and make a world of difference when it comes to sound in your videos. Upgrading your sound could mean less background noise too.

Lighting, location, and background are also important. You want to frame your shot in good light and a good location. It's fine to shoot off the cuff sometimes, but if you're serious about creating quality video, you are going to want to film indoors where you can control the background and lighting. High quality filming lights are available, but you can often recreate this affect in a room with good, bright lighting where you can watch for shadows.

Always be mindful of your background too. One time we shot a series of videos at a desk in an office, only to discover in editing that the paint on the wall behind me was chipped and looked bad. A little prep work can save you time and headaches in the long run.

When developing an equipment list for creating videos, editing software should be near the top. Today's editing tools are easy to learn and use. A small investment in software can save you thousands of dollars in editing costs by a professional. In addition, decent editing will greatly improve the professionalism of your video production. If editing video makes you cringe, get some help. If you're going to be creating videos often, getting educated on editing tools will be worth the time and money. Once you hit the big time you can hire that video and editing crew to handle it.

Lastly, get social with your video logistics. Share a new video with a few friends first. Ask for their feedback. Find some videos you like and ask people what equipment they're using. Go online and price equipment and software. Get educated on the basics before you dive into video. If you're going to do it, do it well. And practice, practice, practice!

Video content

So what kind of content should you put out on YouTube to generate engagement, grow your personal brand, and create more connections? Here are some ideas to get your creative juices flowing.

Topics that your target market is searching for. Think about value you can add by being a solution to what they're looking for. Start with their challenges and create content that provides valuable answers and ideas. Because Google owns YouTube, a video that helps people has the capability of showing up high in a search.

Capitalize on popular subjects. When there are elections, epidemics, and popular news stories, create content that helps people understand what's going on.

Instructional and how-to videos are immensely popular on YouTube. What can you teach your target market? What skills and experience do you have that you can share with others via video?

Product and lifestyle testimonials add credibility and stories to your YouTube channel. Make sure these types of videos are relatable and create empathy. A great testimonial can be very impactful on people.

Demonstrate how to use your product(s) in different ways. Do this in an educational way, not a promotional or pitchy way.

Reviews and interviews can help people, and add another layer of credibility to your channel.

Personal development topics that help people grow or get past an obstacle are memorable. People don't forget who helped them get ahead, even in a small way.

Lifestyle updates can be fun. Sharing your experiences while traveling or getting to do things that most people can't because they're tied to a job can make people want what you have.

APPLICATION:

1. Do you have a desire to create videos? Research the types of content you want to create on YouTube. See what's out there, what you resonates with you, what you can produce.
2. Check your equipment and setting. Be mindful about quality when it comes to lighting and sound, and of course, video quality.
3. Using the ideas in this chapter, brainstorm topics that can grow your personal brand and add value to your target market.
4. Setting up a YouTube account is free, so get started today!

CHAPTER 28: EMAIL MARKETING

Contrary to what you may have heard, email marketing is not dead. It is alive and well, and can produce returns with a great ROI (return on investment).

Email marketing, in fairness to the power of it, could have its own book entirely. In fact, by doing a Google search or a query on Amazon, you will find dozens of websites and books to help you with email marketing.

Effective digital marketing through email requires creating a list through subscribers. Long gone are the days of spam or buying a list and having it be successful. People hold their email sacred now, and revolt against unwanted messages. Email providers are constantly on the hunt for spam in order to keep their users happy.

This is called opt-in, or permission marketing. To do email marketing well, you need to develop a list of contacts with email addresses. You do not need to buy a list. Develop a list by connecting and giving away value.

Great email marketing will happen when you make connections and trust your top priorities. Once you get permission to send someone messages, they will usually welcome them (or at least tolerate them). This is one of the end goals of the **Stop Pitching and Start Connecting** strategy – to be able to market to people because they trust you. We want people to opt-in to what we have to offer. That's when we can get the most out of email marketing.

I've been doing email marketing since 2001, when we had just started to really realize the power of email addresses and were collecting them from our customers and distributors.

At first, like many companies, we started emailing everything all the time. It wasn't unusual for us to send three or four emails a day to our database (not my idea, by the way). However, after hearing the complaints and feedback, I proposed something different. We only emailed people when it was really important, around once a week. All of our other key messaging and updates were put online. Next, we created an opt-in choice for anyone giving us their email address, asking them what types of emails they wanted to receive from us.

This worked well for three reasons. First, it kept our database from ignoring important emails because of being inundated. Second, it pushed traffic to our website and got people using our online tools. Third, it increased our open rate, the percentage of people who actually opened our emails, because they were only receiving emails they wanted.

Once we had established an audience for our emails, we began targeting people through our data and reports. Because we had order details on thousands of people, we could target promotions based on order history. We could promote events to people within a geographic region instead of blanketing the entire list.

This strategy took time to implement and start working, but when it hit its stride, it produced phenomenal results. We were able to backfill sales with offers to people who hadn't ordered in some time. When we sent an important announcement, it no longer got lost in the shuffle. In fact, we went from people either not receiving our emails due to blacklisting (ISPs blocking our emails) or missing them because of the vast amount we sent, to getting calls within seconds when we sent specials, promotions, or news.

The more value we delivered to their inbox with less frequency, the more it increased our open rate and engagement, which led to sales.

I want you to get results with your email marketing as well. You're not a company with a huge database, but you can create an email list based on your online strategy and activities. I want you to grow this list with people who are subscribing. I want people to choose to get email from you.

A good, opt-in email list can be a virtual sales goldmine for your business. When you've done the work of connecting and people want more of what you have to offer, strategic emails can become a drip campaign that ignites the point of sale.

To accomplish this, you need to offer great content that makes you attractive. And, you cannot be pushy, selling constantly, or pitching like a used car salesperson.

It will take a little time to grow your list, but you'll never do it if you don't start and stick with a strategy. You're reading this book for a reason, so let's make the most of it. When you're ready to become an email marketing guru, read more about it, get some training, and ask questions of someone who is really good at it. However, I want to stress that is NEVER too early to start developing an email contact list.

Here are some basic tips for email marketing:

- **Start with a service** that provides great, east-to-use tools for managing a list and creating email campaigns. These services allow you to create forms, emails, and many personalized features. A lot of them have a free program for beginners. A few reputable services to check out include MailChimp, Aweber, Feedburner, and Constant Contact. These sites also offer an incredibly valuable service: they allow you to create email newsletters and campaigns that bypass spam filters and ISP blacklists and hurdles. If you try to send emails to a few hundred people from your Yahoo, Hotmail, or Gmail account, it's going to get blocked most of the time. Your account will be flagged as a spammer and your email marketing will die on the vine. By using a service like MailChimp, your opt-in campaign becomes whitelisted, or approved, and is virtually guaranteed to make it in the email box you're intending. Now whether they open it or not is another story.
- **Create a way to collect email addresses.** If you are blogging, invite people to subscribe. If you have a website, have a form for people to request more information. Create infoproducts you can share for free in exchange for people giving you their email

addresses. Refer to the Ideas chapter near the end of this book to spark your imagination on this.

- **Obtaining email addresses is all about a value proposition or exchange.** In order for people to give you their address, you must offer something they find valuable. Here's where content and connection come into play, big time. When you create a blog that gives people great tips and advice they can apply to their life, they will want to subscribe. When you develop a quick ebook that helps people, they will want to give you their email address in exchange for their free copy. If you put together an informative teleclass or webinar, ask people to give their email when they register. To get value, you must offer value.

- **An example of good email marketing:** I get a Bible verse delivered to my email address every day from Joel Osteen. Since I find the Bible somewhat difficult to understand, getting a verse with a simple explanation of its meaning and how it can apply to my life is very valuable to me. So every day I get this in my email, like clockwork, and I soak it in. Every couple of weeks, I get an email from Joel Osteen offering a DVD or CD package, or one of his books. Do I mind this? Absolutely not. Subconsciously it's a value exchange for me. When I see 'Joel Osteen' in the 'from' area of my inbox, it's welcome. So when he markets to me, it's just part of the equation. And because he's delivering value, I'm much, much more likely to jump at one of his email offers.

- **Subject lines are very important.** I love to subscribe to new emails simply to review what type of subject lines are used. Some grab your attention, others not so much. There are also great books on this. My favorite is *Advertising Headlines That Make You Rich* by David Garfinkel. Bottom line – subject lines matter and can make the difference between someone opening your email or deleting without ever reading it. Give them your attention.

- **Short newsletters** are easily read and digested by most people.

- **Targeted, relevant content is also key.** If someone subscribes to your blog about public speaking and you email them a newsletter about college basketball, they will probably be confused and may unsubscribe altogether. Make sure you are delivering quality, valuable content via email and make it specific to your audience to maintain the connection and trust.

- **Email is a great way to test new material or platforms.** If you typically send your blog and a newsletter via email, try sending a video. Let your audience know they are part of the experiment and give them a way to comment or give you feedback. Marketing becomes simpler when your prospect tells you what they're looking for.

- **Treat your email list like gold**, because it potentially is. Take care of those people. Never abuse the fact that they have given you a piece of who they are – their coveted email address. They are allowing you to enter their inbox, not the other way around.

- **Consider inviting to another value-packed event** instead of pitching with email. If people have subscribed to your content, offer other ways to get more. This will only build trust and get people closer to wanting to take that next step with you.

- **Share useful information with your list.** If you read a great book, promote it to your email list, without an agenda. If you find a great tip or blog, share it with your list. Add value, add value, add value.

- **Continue your education.** Always be learning and evolving your email strategy and content. There are thousands of resources available on email marketing.

Building a successful email list and perfecting your email marketing will take time, but it will be worth it.

Another form of digital marketing – SMS/Text

Another great tool for digital marketing is texting or SMS messaging. Texts are fast and easy to read, and a preferred method of communication for many people. If you're not using texts regularly, it's time to start.

Texts are ideal for team communication and follow up. They are often much less bothersome than a phone call, because someone can respond quickly without leaving the situation they're in.

I'm not going to go into all the tools and strategies for SMS texting, I just want to make sure your mind is open to using this powerful communication method. It's best to communicate with people how they want to be communicated with, and for that alone you should utilize texts as part of your overall strategy.

APPLICATION:

1. Are you building an email list? If not, and you're ready to start, use the information in this chapter and the Ideas chapter to get rolling.
2. Observe the types of emails you receive, especially the subject lines and length of the emails. What appeals to you? Implement any good ideas.
3. If you're serious about email marketing, get more training through a service like Aweber, MailChimp, or Feedburner.

SECTION 7: EXPANDING YOUR REACH THROUGH BLOGS, PODCASTS, AND VIDEOS

Before she ever ran her first marathon, my friend Amanda Murdaugh applied for the New York City Marathon in 2011. That would be a big deal for almost all of us. It has more participants than any marathon in the world, and many consider it to be one of the two best long-distance races on earth.

Applying to run in the New York City Marathon before ever even trying a local marathon is like planning to climb Mt. Everest before you've climbed the highest peak in your state or country.

The task might seem even tougher for someone like Amanda, who after losing 80 pounds in 2010, started running for the first time in her life. Not running marathons, simply running on a treadmill to get into better shape. However, once she discovered her passion and talent for running, she set her sights on what some would consider the epitome of long-distance running.

On November 2, 2014, Amanda finally ran and finished the New York City Marathon. In those three years, motivated by her sister's early death from cancer, she has trained like crazy. She's run multiple marathons and dozens of shorter races. She ran in blistering heat over 100 degrees in the Arizona summer and through cold, wet rain in the winter when she felt like staying on the couch instead.

The entire time she was being guided and driven by a vision to run in the New York City Marathon. The application was submitted. Her belief fueled her determination. Her GPS was set to New York City long before she got there, but by creating that destination, she had direction every single day.

Expanding your reach through your writing, creating a podcast, or recording videos can work the same way. You may not see exactly how you can get there, but create the vision now. Developing content and marketing it in a fun, determined way can build credibility, grow your network, and articulate your expertise and leadership.

Visualization works. I want you to set your GPS now to building a successful platform that helps you grow and meet the right people. Even if you have never written a blog, listened to a podcast, or shot a video, you have what it takes to grab one of these tools and flourish with it. But you must have the belief that you can do so.

Be like Amanda today. Establish a vision to expand your reach online through social media, including your website and a blog of some kind. You see, your faith is always there. It's either working for you or against you. The good news is you get to choose which way the belief wind blows. If you believe you can't create write content that people read, you're right. But if you believe that you are full of valuable expertise and you can learn how to use a platform to provide that value to people, you're also right.

As Jim Collins says in his best-selling book, *Good to Great*, it turns out that greatness isn't a matter of circumstance, it's simply a matter of choice. Choose to be great my friends!

CHAPTER 29: REDEFINING BLOGGING

There are few tools as powerful for connecting and growing your network than a consistent offering of relevant content through blogs, audio podcasts, or videos.

When you think 'blog' you most likely think of a written, article-type post on a web page. The term 'blog' is defined by Google as a regularly updated website or web page that is written in a conversational or informal style. For this book, however think about a 'blog' and 'blogging' as written blogs, audio podcasts, and videos. I'm lumping all three of them together under the blogging umbrella. This section will educate you on these tools, open your mind to different ways to expand your reach, and help you choose the method right for you.

While all three of these are somewhat different animals, they all can be used with a similar mentality to a written blog. In addition, each of them can be utilized to market your content and personal brand. Think of them like a family. A spoon, knife, and fork are all eating utensils. Each has its benefits, uses, pros, and cons. Writing, podcasts, and videos can work in the same fashion.

I've worked with many people who think that they have to have a written blog, but they hate writing. Or, they've been told they should have a YouTube video channel, but they aren't really passionate about creating videos. And many people are unfamiliar with podcasts altogether.

By giving you the basics of each tool, you can make a better decision about which one will be a good fit for you. If you dislike writing, a written blog probably isn't for you. However, you can create videos or audio podcasts using the same mentality as a written blog.

Let's define all three mediums and then dive into each in a little more detail so that you can make a more informed choice on which type of "blog" is best for you.

Written blogs: The traditional weblog you read online. Generally, these types of blogs are posted directly to the author's website or a guest host website.

Podcasts: This is an audio blog, created from the terms 'iPod' and 'broadcast'. The author records their topic and content in an auditory format, usually an mp3 file. Podcasts can be uploaded to iTunes AND placed on the recorder's website, just like a written blog. There are also other websites that host podcasts, like Hipcast or Libsyn.

If you've never listened to a podcast, I highly encourage you to jump on iTunes and search for a topic of interest. Just like written blogs, there are podcasts for almost every topic and passion. I've been a big fan of podcasts for years. One major benefit is the ability to download them to your iPod, computer, or phone and listen to them while offline or when you don't have access to the internet. A great time to listen to a podcast is while you're driving, similar to listening to the radio.

Videos: Videos that act like written blogs are sometimes called Vlogs. For this book, I'm writing about any video you record to market your brand, content, products, etc. Like the other two types of blogs, videos can be uploaded directly to a personal website. They can also be uploaded and housed on video sites like YouTube or Vimeo. Videos are not limited to you appearing on camera, simply talking. There are simple tools you can use to create videos out of powerpoint presentations, animations, or a mix of talking head, slides, stats, photos, and other information.

Websites

Before we go further about why have a blog (remember this includes podcasts and videos), pros and cons of the different types of blogs, content ideas, and more, let's discuss **your website.** If you are able to have your own personal website to host your blog, I highly recommend it.

You can get a free website through Wordpress, Blogger, Weebly, or any number of other free services to get started. Of course, you can use a paid service and host if you wish, as well as pay someone to design your website.

This book is NOT about creating your website; it's about using social media effectively and developing your personal brand online. I will offer a few tips based on my experience, but this is most definitely not a website book. There are enough books and information online to help you in that area, so I'm going to focus on your social networking strategy.

If you decide to go with the free website option, I strongly recommend you get your own domain name. Having your own domain name makes it easier for people to find your website and could show people you're serious about your personal brand and web presence. Most free website services offer an option to purchase a domain name to be associated with your site, well worth the small investment.

CHAPTER 30: WHY HAVE A BLOG?

*A blog is a great thing to build a business around, or to help bring more exposure to an already existing business. If you already have a business, start writing relevant blog posts, information, or tips that will be useful and helpful to your potential or current customers/clients. Blogs are a great way to get your customers to come to your website and **keep you on their minds.*** - Lisha Yost, Founder of Blog and Retire University.

I'm a big fan of blogging. I read blogs every day. I love to write blogs. I listen to podcasts. The immense value I've received from this medium cannot be measured. I've also remarked how videos have helped me learn new skills, including how to edit audio using Audacity.

If you've ever wanted to start a blog (Remember I'm combining written blogs, podcasts, and videos into this section, all under the 'blogging' umbrella.), then let me demystify the process and help you get started, TODAY.

Let's start with the **benefits** of having a blog.

Build credibility

As I've mentioned, articulating your expertise is key to getting noticed and making connections. Putting your tips, experiences, stories, and advice in print, audio, or video, builds credibility. It becomes real to people. Since most people will NEVER start any kind of blog, you set yourself apart by creating it and following through.

When a prospect is able to see your website and a history of blogs, it becomes an extension of your business card. When you post something on social media about your business, your acumen, your experience, or any kind of invitation, your blog adds major credibility. By showing you are an authority on a topic, you reach peoples' subconscious mind, where decisions are made.

Adding value to the world builds a layer of credibility with people as well. By creating some kind of blog that gives away value, you are developing trust. "Your blog is your voice," says blogger Geoff Talbot. "It reflects who you are and when it is used correctly, it can really connect you to a large audience in cyberspace."

Creative outlet

It's easy to fall into the self-made trap of saying, "I'm not creative." Let's eliminate that type of negative self-talk! I'm speaking from personal experience because I used to that person. I used to think, "I don't have good ideas," and "I'm not a creative person." Creativity is in everyone, it's just a matter of how you define it.

We are all creative beings. You don't have to be an artist to be creative. Even the most logical, mathematical mind creates. Where an artist uses creativity to express worldview or beauty, logical minds often use it to solve problems or design new products. Take a minute to think about your creativity. Remember the times when you came up with a solution or a workaround to a challenge. You are unique and have a valuable message to share. You don't have to paint on a canvas to produce something new.

But how can potential prospects and connections see your creativity? Through some kind of blog. How can you communicate your opinions, give practical advice, and express creativity in a forum to get noticed? A blog. How can you inspire others and spread your vision? Start a blog.

"I like blogging because it's an easy way to help people and get your ideas out, and sporadically and strategically broadcast about new products or services," says Lisha Yost.

Gain followers/subscribers/connections

If you are consistent, fresh, and genuine with your blog outlet, it inevitably will lead to more followers, likes, connections, and subscribers.

There are millions of blogs out there. How will you stand out? By being yourself and sharing your experiences. When you blog in your niche and expertise, you will attract new connections you never would have met without your blog.

"With my blog, I have been able to develop a deeper connection with like-minded individuals," says Stacie Theis. "People like to share their experiences and ideas. Asking them to be a part of your blog through interviews or guest posts is a great way to open doors. I have met hundreds of authors by simply offering to interview them for my blog. People are also willing to share your blog posts, about them, on their social media sites and/or their own blog which in turn gives you great exposure."

Win-win!

Your writing skills will improve

If you choose to start a written blog, it will force you to become a better writer. Writing a blog will challenge your writing skills and compel you to grow every time you write.

As with any new skill, it gets easier as you do it consistently. Those first few blog posts may feel like pulling teeth, but as you develop a schedule and stick to it, your creativity shows up more consistently, too. The posts become easier to write. Often ideas pile up in your mind, just waiting to be expressed, and when they don't, you can visit other blogs to get the juices flowing. Or maybe you need some white space to open your mind to the possibilities. Author Anne Lamont says if you're going to create, you have to make time to stare out the window.

Provide a service

What's missing in the world today? What did you need that you couldn't find? Starting a blog could provide a service that fills a void. Your tips, advice, and how-to blogs can provide a service that your target market could really use.

"I started blogging about Pinterest because I needed help and I realized a lot of others did too. I started helping people and using screen shots to teach people," says Michelle Held.

Help others

Have you heard the saying, a rising tide raises all ships? Well, you can be the tide that raises those boats. Helping others creates a magnetic effect, drawing people to you. When you give value to someone that they implement, they don't forget you. You can probably remember the person who gave you a big break, the person who taught you how to ride a bike, or the mentor who gave you the inspiration to chase your dreams.

Helping people will never go out of style. The world could always use more of it. Your blog can be the catalyst to impact many lives.

Why are you interested in having a blog?

This is a tough question for most people. I've had many, many networkers tell me they wanted to start a blog and ask me for help. My first question is always, "Why do you want to have a blog?"

If their answer is that they don't know, they're just 'supposed to', or they just want to make money with a blog, I tell them to go back to the drawing board.

 "First you need to know why you're starting the blog and your objective of the blog." says Lisha Yost. "Know what topics you should be and will be covering (and why)—things you're passionate about, things you're learning a lot about, things you know a lot about."

You will never keep a blog going consistently, give it your all, or enjoy it if you don't have a "why." No one is forcing you to create a blog. You have to be self-inspired and know why you are doing it. Something inside has to drive you to do the work.

Luke Dancy says, "Blogging is a great way to provide content to support what you do and talk about something you enjoy. **Content is king** online and what you write can't be found anywhere else! The more you can 'give' your customers in the form of entertainment, facts, or something funny, the less they will feel pressured when you go in for the sell. If someone learns a lot from you on a consistent basis the least they can do is buy your product. Blogging also gives your brand a true 'voice' so people can get a more personal look at who and what you are."

APPLICATION:

1. Open your mind to different types of blogs. If you want a written blog, read a few this week. If you're interested in podcasts, download one from iTunes today. If it's videos you want to create, jump on YouTube and see what type of videos there are and what interests you.
2. Why do you want to have a blog? Get down to the core reason that will make you want to blog weekly. How will it help people?
3. What potential benefits would help you build your business or personal brand?

CHAPTER 31: BLOGGING MYTHS AND MISCONCEPTIONS

There are many misconceptions about blogs, bloggers, and blogging. (Remember, for the purpose of this book we're lumping written blogs, podcasts, and videos together under the labels of blogs and blogging.) Here are a few common blogging myths:

1. You can make lots of money with a blog, very quickly

There are a lot of people who make money with their blog. However, they worked very hard on it for many years. They were consistent. They posted when they didn't feel like it – when they weren't inspired, when they were on vacation, and when they were sick.

You CAN make money with your blog, but the more likely result is that you will grow an audience and your blog will be a part of your online platform.

The thought that you write a blog and the money will follow is only true if you do the right things. Be consistent. Provide value. Market yourself. Promote others.

Blogging can be a great addition to your overall strategy, but if you're only doing it to make money, you will probably be frustrated.

"The 'show me the money' attitude won't work," says pro Cliff Ravenscraft.

2. You have to blog daily for it to work

Blogging daily is great, but not necessary. It's more important to blog consistently. Set a schedule you can actually keep. I've worked with LOTS of networkers who start a blog and create a blogging schedule that's ridiculously hard to maintain.

183

If you can only post something once a week, start there. Ramp it up to twice or three times a week after that. If you try to keep too rigorous a schedule, you will give up or become burned out before your blog can grow legs.

3. Anyone can start a blog

This is also true, but very few people are actually willing to do what it takes to maintain these blogs. So while anyone can start a blog, very few will be around in a year. Most will quit after 90 days or less.

4. It's easy to get lots of subscribers

Huge myth. Getting subscribers takes consistency, solid content, networking, promoting, and meeting the right people. It also takes good technology to capture subscribers efficiently. Bloggers who have lots of subscribers worked very, very hard at it. More importantly, they focused on serving the subscribers they do have, no matter how many. Quality over quantity. "The question you should be asking is, 'How do I build a deeper relationship with people who are already listening?'" says Cliff Ravenscraft.

5. You have to be passionate about writing

Not true. My friend Geoff Talbot writes a blog called Seven Sentences (SevenSentences.com) that only contains – you guessed it – seven sentences. Many other blogs will only have a couple of sentences when they have a quick point to get across.

You don't need to be an English major to write a blog either. Most popular blogs are written in a more conversational tone.

If you don't like to write, you probably should NOT have a written blog. Create podcasts or videos instead. Create a pictorial blog and promote it with Instagram or Pinterest. Open your mind to a different kind of blog if writing isn't your thing.

6. Blogging/podcasting/recording videos takes a lot of time

I can write a short blog, post it to my website, and get the word out using Hootsuite in less than 20 minutes. If you struggle with writing or you like to write long blogs, then blogging may take a lot of time. But it doesn't have to. You can record a five minute video or podcast and have it posted online in less than 20 minutes. Most of us could find time for writing, podcasting, or video creation if we really want to.

7. Blogging won't last – it's here today, gone tomorrow

Blogging has been around for a long time. The current format of a weblog is newer compared to other outlets, but blogging is not going way. Change and evolve? Yes. Gone tomorrow? I wouldn't bet on it.

8. You have to spend a lot of money to create a blog

You can start a blog in the next five minutes, absolutely free. Really. There are multiple sites that will give you a free blogging website that actually looks good. This is a great way to get your feet wet blogging. YouTube is free and you can upload audio to iTunes and several other sites, 100% free. Upgrade to a paid service when you're ready. Once you get the hang of it, you can spend money on ads, SEO, or web design, if you decide to.

Design and appearance won't mean much if you don't determine your voice and create good content. Most great blogs started out simple without spending much, if any money on design. According to Geoff Talbot, "The biggest mistake people make is that they are super focused on design (the outward appearance) without giving enough thought to the character, the nature, the real identity of their voice. They end up with something that looks good but is dull to consume."

APPLICATION:

1. What objections or misconceptions do you have about blogging? Write them down and then let them go. If you have a desire to start blogging (writing, podcasting or creating videos), just do it.
2. Talk to bloggers. Ask them why they do it.

3. If you're ready to start a blog, take action. Even if you simply open up a document on your computer and compose a blog or two, it's better than waiting. If you want to record videos or podcasts, you can create a quick outline of your first episode.

CHAPTER 32: WHICH TYPE OF BLOG IS RIGHT FOR YOU?

Hopefully you've already started seeing yourself in one or more of the blogging options. Think about not only your personal preference (which way do YOU best receive information, through reading? Listening? Watching?), but also about your skills, talents, and schedules. Keep that in mind as you consider the pros and cons of each medium.

Written blogs

Pros:

- Easy to read from any internet connection.
- Widely available.
- Quick prep and upload time.
- Great creative outlet for writers.
- Also great for people who like to read.
- Only equipment needed is a computer or tablet, which most of us have.

Cons:

- Rely on people visiting your site or receiving an email.
- Writing consistently can be challenging.
- Auditory and visual learners may not be in tune with your material.
- The written word does not always convey your passion like audio or video.
- Lots of competition.

Podcasts

Listening to podcasts can help you. But what about recording your own podcast? If you enjoy speaking, they could be a good fit for you.

They also can have high impact and loyalty. "You're in their ear, and you're talking one on one with people," says JB Glossinger, who makes his living with his daily podcasts. "There's just something about that intimate relationship that you create that isn't there with video. Speaking into somebody's ear or on their speakers in their car, that just creates a really interesting bond."

I can attest to this bond that gets created. There are many times when I feel like JB is talking directly to me and no one else. I feel like he wrote this content and recorded it just for me. It was a message I really needed to hear. Many people feel this way about podcasts and podcasters. Wouldn't that be a great thing to happen to you and your business?

"With podcasting, people give me more of their time and attention," says Cliff Ravenscraft. "With an audio podcast, when people feel like they know you and trust you, they listen to every minute."

Bruce Van Horn advises, "Try to communicate with people in the ways they want to be communicated with. There's a certain percentage of the population that wants to get their information audibly. Podcasts reach those people."

If you are already familiar with podcasts, or you see their value, and you are starting a blog, consider a podcast. If you're dedicated and willing to be persistent and consistent, you may be able to turn a podcast into a self-generated, endless warm market funnel.

Pros:

- People hear your voice, literally. Your voice can create a very strong connection with people.
- You can stress what you mean without leaving it to interpretation that comes with reading.
- Does not require much writing and no writing that people will see.
- Works great for auditory learners.

- Less competition than videos and written blogs.

Cons:

- Requires recording equipment. You can get this equipment inexpensively (like a free app on your phone). However, creating a quality recording to generate an audience and sound professional will require an investment, anywhere from $99-$5,000.
- Can require more time to absorb than a written blog. If your audience has limited time, they may not be into a podcast.
- Can take more prep time than a written blog.

Videos

Pros:

- Your audience gets to see your beautiful face *and* hear your gorgeous voice.
- Works for both auditory and visual learners.
- Expensive equipment is not necessary in the beginning. User-driven content is big, so using your smart phone may be acceptable, depending on your audience.
- Less competition than a written blog.

Cons:

- Requires production/editing time and some technical knowledge to be done well.
- Content can be difficult to create consistently.
- Many people get bored with 'talking head' videos, so creativity is a must.
- More competition than a podcast.

What are your passions/strengths/expertise?

"Is writing your strength or do you communicate better verbally? Are you good on camera?" asks Geoff Talbot. "It is important to choose your most effective mode of communication, rather than just doing what you've been told."

Whichever way you choose to expand your reach online, it should tap into your passions, strengths, and expertise. When you write or record from your area of expertise, it shows. When you are excited about something, you stand out. When you give value based on your strengths, you become attractive.

Many new bloggers make the mistake of blogging about a topic they want to be an expert in, but they have very little experience. If you're just starting to build your online platform, providing online marketing tips you take from another site simply will not work. Stick to your expertise. People want to hear it.

If you want to start a blog, make a list of the things you are passionate about and have experience in. Then, determine which of these themes you would want to blog about. Ask yourself, will people actually care about it?

What can you do consistently?

Steve Gutzler says, "The secret formula is consistency, being very relevant, and doing your very best to create content and value that's attractive."

Hopefully you have learned that consistency is critical in all areas of social media. This is especially true with your blog. "Staying consistent as part of your strategy is really the only way to build a true following and have people care," says Luke Dancy.

Would you subscribe to a magazine that went to print sporadically? They come out three months in a row, disappear for two months, back for one month, then gone for three months. You'd never stand for that. You would cancel your subscription immediately.

When people find something they like, they want to know how to get it consistently and repeatedly. You can write the best blog this week, that five people love, but if you are absent next week, those five people are gone.

Each time you stop or post erratically, you're like a car going from stoplight to stoplight. A car uses the most gas when accelerating from a stop. It's fuel efficient when it's on the freeway, doing 65 miles per hour.

The way you choose to communicate or market your content works the same way. If you're stopping and starting, momentum will be impossible to generate. You've got to get that blog on the freeway. You've got to become predictable and scheduled when it comes to frequency of your posts (but not necessarily the quality or style of your content).

Create a schedule you can stick to. Then stick to it. It doesn't matter if you have zero subscribers. Post on schedule. All the time. This is why it's so important to create a posting timeline you can actually meet.

Many people start diets, right? Yet many overweight people never meet their goals. One of the reasons is they set expectations they cannot possibly meet. They haven't exercised in years, yet they plan on running five days a week. Once they get a week or two in and start experiencing failure, they give up entirely. Their initial excitement and motivation get flushed down the toilet and their cycle of staying unfit continues.

This is what I see with people starting a blog or new social media accounts. They are excited. They see the value. They know it's something they should do. They can feel that it can make a difference in the long run. Yet, they set expectations, whether it's a crazy posting schedule or anticipated results, and they quit before they ever get to the sweet spot.

Don't let that be you. You can do this. But be prepared. Commit to starting a blog and keeping a simple schedule for the next 12 months. That's right, **a full year**. Try one day a week to start. If you can do that for 12 weeks, then bump it up to twice a week. If that feels good, try three times a week.

APPLICATION:

1. Ready to get started? Visit StopPitching.com/Resources to download the blogging checklist. Create a schedule you can stick to. The checklist will work with written blogs, audio podcasts, and videos.

2. For more information on blogging, whether it's written, audio, or video, visit StopPitching.com/Resources and download the free ebook with every interview from the book you're reading.

3. Get familiar with whichever medium interests you. If you like to write, read and subscribe to written blogs. If podcasts might work for you, download a few and research hardware you might need to record audio. If it's video you want to produce, watch videos to see what gets views and what intrigues you.

4. If you're interested in creating your own podcast, visit PodcastAnswerMan.com and check out Cliff's Podcasting A-Z course.

CHAPTER 33: WHAT ARE YOUR BLOGGING GOALS?

This is similar to 'why do you want to blog?' from earlier. You need to have goals. Your goals need to be achievable and smart. "Making money from a blog" is not a goal. It's a wish.

- Good starting goals look like this:
- Create a list of topics and keep growing it.
- Post once a week (or more) for 90 days.
- Write one guest blog a month.
- Promote your blog once or twice a day on Twitter and twice a week on Facebook.
- Invite friends to read/watch/listen and comment on your blog.
- Review your site traffic and subscribers at the end of each month. Adapt your blogging schedule accordingly.

My point is simple – you need to have a few goals. Not a ton. One or two will suffice to get started. Three is great. Give yourself some simple milestones to reach. You can always create bigger goals down the road.

Like the serial dieter, too many goals or too lofty of goals will cause you to quit. Start out simple and build momentum. Let's get that car on the freeway!

Be time efficient

Blogging does not need to take a lot of time. Let's say you are posting twice a week. If it's a written blog, you can create content in about an hour, so we'll assume two hours – an hour a blog post. If you're posting a podcast or video, we will assume the same timeframe.

Next, you need to publish or post it, then promote it. If you are using the right tools, your weekly promotion scheduling shouldn't take more than 30 minutes a week.

That's a total of two and a half hours a week. And I'm being very liberal. You could cut that time in half with a little experience. I currently spend less than two hours a week on TWO different blogs, plus all my social media.

Let's see...there are 168 hours in a week. If you want it badly enough, you will find the few hours it takes to produce your blog.

Here's what I've seen from some networkers. They use their blog/podcast/YouTube channel as their work for the day. It becomes a *time waster* so they don't have to work on prospecting, connecting, or following up. They think, "Oh, I wrote my blog for today. I'm done. Time well spent. I don't need to do anything else except wait for the checks to roll in."

This couldn't be further from the truth. Your blog is like a business card. You can update it as often as you want, but it can't do anything by itself. Your blog is just part of your overall platform. Without connecting, promoting, and prospecting, your blog will have a tough time growing legs.

Blogging should be something you have a passion for – something you really like to do. If you are only doing it because you think you have to or you think it will turn into an ATM, it's not for you.

If you're ready to share your expertise with the world, give away great value, and attract new connections through a creative outlet, then you are ready to start a blog.

APPLICATION:

1. What are your blogging goals? Use the blogging worksheet at StopPitching.com/Resources to create realistic goals for your blog. Revisit these goals often. Course corrections are normal.
2. Create a time each week when you can create content for a written blog, podcast, or video. Make it a priority.

3. Get help when you need it. Have someone review your posts for spelling and punctuation. Ask friends to read your blog and comment.
4. Connect with someone who can help mentor you. Talk to a podcaster, a YouTuber, or blogger about their experiences and advice.

CHAPTER 34: BLOGGING TIPS AND IDEAS

Let's get you moving forward! Here are practical tips and ideas you can apply right away. I also want to get your creative juices flowing. One of my strengths is helping people brainstorm content creation and design an online platform that will work for them. It's fun to get people believing they can create great content and excited that they can tap into their passion and expertise to develop their personal brand. When they realize they can actually ENJOY the process, that's when the momentum propels them forward.

Creating written, audio, or video content

So you have the right mentality to start a blog. Now where do you come up with content to post once a week or more?

This stumps a lot of people. They may have some mojo and get a couple blogs done, then realize blogging takes effort, work, and perseverance. Don't fret though. I guarantee you have enough content to get started and maintain a rewarding blog.

You don't have to come up with 200 blogs today. Content will come to you as you get inspired in daily life. As you learn things about your business and grow, you will come up with stories, tips, advice, and content that people will want to read, hear, or watch. This is why it is important to blog about something you have experience in or some level of expertise. Take a deep breath and trust this process. You have enough content to create something awesome. I know it.

Personal experiences or stories

Start with a list of personal experiences and stories that have a lesson. Humility is great when it comes to relaying experiences. People want to know you're human. Humility also creates **empathy**, which is the most powerful force in marketing.

When people see that you were in a sticky situation, made mistakes, and persevered, they can live through you and gain inspiration for their own lives. Think back to the value you can share, from lessons learned, how to avoid mistakes, and how you accomplished something. Make a list of experiences that you can write or talk about.

Be careful about talking about yourself too much, though. Your personal stories must be broadcasted in a way that provides value and application. Work your stories into tips, advice, lists, and lessons that people can apply. Ask questions and challenge people with your experiences.

All stories should have some level of the basic building blocks – a hero, a villain, a climax, and a victory.

"The most common mistake with blogging, however, is that people write or create content about themselves expecting that others will naturally be interested," explains Geoff Talbot. " It's very important to create content for others in a powerful way that enables and invites connection. Engagement is guaranteed when we can take all our attention off ourselves and place it on our intended with much love and appreciation." It's all in the presentation. You can share personal stories, but have a purpose and a takeaway for your reader.

As I've mentioned before, the best way to learn is to observe. Read other blogs, listen to podcasts, or watch others' videos. See what you like. What draws you in? What are people subscribing to and why? You never know what might inspire you or help you become more creative.

Comment on current events/news

This type of material can be very timely and attractive. However, avoid talking politics or religion, or being divisive. Instead, take a contrary point of view that has a business, personal development, or educational spin to it. Get creative with your topics and titles so you can attract your target market.

Instructional/how-to

This is a very popular subject area. The internet has made it easier than ever to learn how to do almost anything.

Start a list of things you can teach others through your blog. Don't discount your experience. What may seem ordinary, simple, or basic to you might be the knowledge that could help thousands of people.

My good friend and real estate pro Becca Atterberry told me, "We don't know what we know." Meaning, we know so much that we often take it for granted. Just because I know how to use Hootsuite quickly and easily, doesn't mean it comes that easy to others. You probably have a lot of knowledge and skills that you take for granted.

When creating this type of content, try making it evergreen, meaning it is still useful a year from now, two years from now, etc. That way people will want to come back to it.

How-to videos, audios, and written blogs are literally limitless in possibilities. Instructional blogs provide a great opportunity to passively market your business and products. Let me get your brain going with some examples.

- o How to make sure you stay healthy on the road
- o 5 ways supplements help busy parents
- o How to structure your day for the most productivity
- o How to create additional income in your spare time
- o How to choose the right business to start from home
- o 7 ideas to get more family time

Make sure your instructional blogs are NOT only about passively marketing your business and/or products. Follow an 80/20 rule on this (or our trusty 90/10 rule). Make at least 80% of your how to blogs about simply helping people and providing useful information; less than 20% about passively promoting. If people feel like you are PITCHING through your blog, they will tune out.

Remember, people have a sixth sense when it comes to being sold or pitched. They avoid it like the plague. They want to join something or buy from someone they trust. They want to belong. Endless prospecting through your videos, podcast, or writing will turn people OFF.

Recipes

Recipes have become one of the top searches on the web. You can capitalize on this popularity by posting your favorite recipes, especially if they have a unique twist. It fits perfectly if you are working with a company that sells nutritional, weight loss, or food products.

Don't post recipes if they don't fit into what your blog is about or if you're not passionate about them. Posting recipes just to tap into their status online won't work. If recipes are going to be part of your strategy, then post them at least once a week.

Take a look at what others are doing with recipes. You may not want to include them in your blog at all, but instead create a recipe area on your website. That way people can get great value from your website and passively find your blog.

A note about including your products in your recipes. It's a very smart thing to do. But try to follow an 80/20 rule with this too. If all your recipes have your products in them, people will be confused and be turned off. You want to generate curiosity in a genuine way.

When you post four great recipes that people are checking out and the fifth contains one of your products, people will ask you about them. They will want to know where they can get them. BOOM!

You see, strategy is always in play. Pitching a lot, even passively, will hold you back from reaching your potential. Instead, make selling a byproduct of your online platform. When your agenda is simply to help people and provide outstanding value, you will attract more. When people start asking you questions, it gets fun.

Inspiration

Inspirational and motivational material will never go out of style. This is a topic that you can continually build on as your blog evolves. If you decide to write inspirational posts, try to work them around your personal experiences or stories that resonate with you.

Reviews

Book reviews. Product reviews. Film reviews. Travel reviews. Business reviews. The list of things to review goes on and on. I like reviews because they allow you to promote someone else's material while attracting a larger audience.

My wife Stacie started her blog by reviewing children's books. She had written a children's book and had a hard time getting it published. So she started reviewing books and interviewing their authors (more on that next). People loved her reviews and the FREE publicity she was offering. As her following grew, she no longer had to ask people to review their books or interview them. They started contacting her, requesting to have their book reviewed and posted on her blog.

With reviews, you want to be careful to be honest yet not be negative. Obviously you don't want to post that you love every chapter of every book or you love every product you review. However, if you post too much negativity, people won't want you to review what they have to offer.

Interviews

Interviews are a fantastic way to subconsciously be associated with other experts, therefore be considered an expert yourself. Think about people who became 'experts' and made a name for themselves simply by interviewing other people:

- Oprah Winfrey
- Larry King

- Howard Stern
- David Letterman
- Malcolm Gladwell
- Jim Collins
- Barbara Walters
- The list goes on and on and on.

My wife differentiated herself from other reviewers by incorporating an interview with the author as part of her review.

Someone who helped me with this book, Joshua Sprague, wrote a book (*SMASH! Break Through Your Productivity Barriers With Proven Secrets From Top 6 & 7 Figure Infopreneurs*) where he interviewed other successful people. This became a top seller on Amazon. John Lee Dumas started his *Entrepreneur On Fire* podcast where he simply interviews all sorts of entrepreneurs in a way that inspires and helps others take action on their goals.

One of the great things about interviews is that you can make them any percentage of your strategy. You can interview people for all your blogs or one blog a month. I started interviewing people regularly for my "Limitless" blog series and podcast, which people loved and were very eager to be interviewed for.

That's another good thing about interviews – people love to be interviewed! This means you can grow your network and meet new people by requesting to interview them. This allows you to get to know and help them by promoting what they are all about.

People are going to your website/podcast/YouTube channel to get these interviews, so you become associated with the expertise of your interviewee. Think about it. No one questions Oprah's background, education, or experience. That's because subconsciously they link her with the people she's talking to. I've actually heard this called the 'Oprah Effect.' People believe you are an expert because you're doing the interviewing.

I encourage you to interview people regularly, whether you feature them on your blog or not. You will meet some great people and learn things you never would have otherwise.

Lists

Lists are very popular with bloggers and blog readers. They are easy to read, quick to digest, and are a natural way that people make decisions. Think about it – most of us make lists every day. What to buy at the store. To-do lists for work. A list of school supplies. Bills to be paid. Even if they are just mental lists, people can handle a simple list of advice, tips, or things to do. Lists are also something that you can create very quickly, even from your phone.

Some examples of lists:

- 5 ways to spend more time with your kids
- 4 lessons I learned while sitting in Starbucks
- 7 reasons to start a home based business
- 3 things all entrepreneurs should do to start their day
- 5 books you can't live without
- The case for and against organic eating

Writers have created entire books out of a list. My friend Stephen Shapiro wrote *Best Practices Are Stupid: 40 Ways to Out-Innovate the Competition*. The chapters are literally divided into 40 tips and ideas to help companies create more innovation.

Guest posts from others

Inviting other bloggers to write posts (or video/audio) for your blog can take some pressure off you to create content 100% of the time. Having guests on your blog is a win-win. You promote them, they promote you, and it's a great way to get to know people. Guest posts can also add credibility to your site.

Encouraging other people to guest blog on your site isn't something you need to do as a new blogger and it's not something you absolutely have to do, ever.

First you need to focus on why you want a blog, developing your own content, marketing your blog, etc. There will be time later to invite guests or guest blog down the road.

Partnerships/promote others

Strategic partnerships can be very helpful. For example, you can write a blog about someone's online business in exchange for them including a link to your site in their weekly newsletter.

Promoting businesses and people you believe in is a healthy strategy. When you find something good, tell the world about it. (Word-of-mouth advertising!)

Keep it brief whenever possible

Brevity is essential with blogs. It's okay to be a little longer once you have an audience, but start short.

How short? Do some research on what's already out there. If you're going to start a home-based business podcast for moms, go in iTunes and find out how long those types of podcasts are. Read some popular blogs to get a feel for length. Watch a few videos to learn more about how long they should be. Length also depends on your target market and their attention span.

Make sure you're comfortable and consistent. If you can't come up with 10 minutes worth of audio, then make your podcast shorter.

Here's my point: you can't go wrong with keeping it brief. Most people are NOT going to spend 30 minutes listening or watching anything when it's new to them, and most people don't enjoy long written articles on-line either. The exception is when you have developed trust with your audience or when you can be extremely engaging. As your audience grows, you will get a feel for when you can create longer posts or recordings that still keep people absorbed.

I know a great networker with years of experience and knowledge. Enough knowledge to create a killer blog that most of us would envy. He's a good writer, and he's articulate. He's good with people, likeable, and a good storyteller.

When he started his blog, he simply couldn't keep it brief. He would write three to four pages of material for one blog. Even after I edited it down, there would still be pages and pages of material.

I told him his blogs had to be shorter, or no one would want to read them. I advised he would get burnt out writing them too. Sure enough, after about seven blogs, he had very few subscribers, very few site visits, and he was struggling to write novellas for a blog.

There's a reason why all TED talks are 18 minutes or less. Attention spans in today's always on, technology everywhere society are getting reduced by the day. Distractions are all around us. If you want to be heard, start by keeping it shorter rather than longer.

Keep it conversational

A simple way to keep your written blogs brief is by using short, punchy sentences. Perfect sentences and English are not required. Yes, you want to make sure your spelling is correct and you have decent use of punctuation, but some grammar rules can be thrown out the window. You don't need fully constructed sentences. We're not trying to make your high school English teacher proud; we're trying to connect with people.

Like Thomas Edison said, "There are no rules here. We're trying to accomplish something." Take a conversational tone with your blogs – all kinds, written, audio, or video.

Keep it simple

This is important. Creating complicated videos or writing long-winded stories won't win over your target audience. A blog can be one minute of video. Three minutes of audio. A few sentences. Keep in mind this is a suggestion, not the rule.

Simple, easy to digest, and actionable blogs get the most attention. Be helpful and educate people and they will find value in your work.

Links to add value/relevance

For written blogs, you will want to use links whenever it makes sense. If you are reviewing books, link to the site where the reader can buy them. If you are referring to another website or blog, include a link.

Adding links adds relevance and can be another way for you to passively market your business and/or products. For example, if you are posting a recipe for a smoothie and it includes protein powder you distribute, make that listing a link to your website where the reader can get more information and BUY.

Ask questions

Remember the power of asking questions. Stephen Shapiro says if you want better answers, ask better questions. Luke Dancy repeatedly trains people to ask questions in their Facebook posts. I have always trained people to open presentations with a question to engage people immediately. Questions beg the subconscious to answer. They make great headlines and get your audience thinking.

Break up longer posts with images

Pictures and images are eye candy that allows you to break up your written blog posts. They also subconsciously speak and can help relay your message no matter the venue. Get in the habit of taking pictures with your phone and find a good photo/image site to use for your blogs. You can also learn to create or use simple, useful infographics.

Learn and use social media daily to promote your blog

When I asked blogging pro Lisha Yost about the biggest mistake people make with their blog, her answer was simple and profound. She said, "They don't market their blogs enough or correctly."

Use social media daily to connect with people and organically promote your blog. Facebook is great for informing your current network about your blog posts. Twitter can help you reach like-minded connections and get noticed by new people. Pinterest works for those who like visuals.

Social media is such an easy way to market yourself, but you've got to use it consistently, every day. Not every site. Not hours and hours. Only 20 minutes a day of focused time will make a big difference.

Bonus Tips

I asked blogger Geoff Talbot to give us his best tips on expanding your reach through blogging.

Blogging tips from Geoff Talbot:

DO:

- Write or speak from your heart and don't try to censor what you are trying to say in your first draft.
- Imagine one person and create a blog post or a video just for them (without mentioning who they are, of course).
- Ask questions and create a narrative that takes people on some kind of journey.
- Look at how the rest of the people in your niche are behaving online and do the opposite.
- Always listen, always learn, always try to engage.

DO NOT:

- o Sign up for an online program that promises you success but does not spend a significant portion of time helping you find your voice.
- o Try to follow a formula then expect success.
- o Try to sell a product or service directly through your blog. Instead use it to build relationships.
- o Do not write a blog as though it is a thesis; write as though it is a conversation instead.

APPLICATION:

1. What ideas excite you? Reviews, lists, how-to, or interviews? Whatever it is, start brainstorming how you can take action. Who can you interview? What do you want to review? What type of how-to blogs can you create?
2. If you need further inspiration or brainstorming, dive into the medium you are looking to create. Read, listen to, or watch posts that resonate with you, determine why you like them, and what you can do with your content.
3. Your blog does not need to be perfect. Going after perfection will lead to inaction. Be yourself and add value to people. Above all, just get started!

CHAPTER 35: GETTING STARTED WITH A BLOG

"Just start a blog, it isn't hard. My daughter helped me pick a URL and set it up in WordPress. Just set it up, pick a template, and you're off and running. You can have a blog in a day. Push it out on your social media. The first time you write a blog, maybe only one person sees it. Who cares? Be consistent, be in it, jump in." –Chris Freytag

Getting started is easy. Don't overcomplicate this or let any fear of technology hold you back.

Quick reminder: by 'blog' I'm talking about the creative outlet that fits you best – writing, audio, or video.

There was a time when you didn't know how to use a computer, the internet, or your smartphone. There have been a lot of challenges you have overcome and new things you have learned and mastered. Blogging is no different. Relax and trust that you can do this if you want it badly enough.

Remember to think big picture. Your blog won't become an overnight success. You may not have a thousand subscribers in 30 days. This is going to take work, which is why you need to pick a topic and type of blog that will excite you on the days when no one reads your blog or life seems to get in the way.

First, decide on a medium or format. Written blog, podcast, or video series? What can you do consistently? Maybe some sort of combination? What will you love to do even if you get zero subscribers in 90 days?

Pick a theme and start to create content. This isn't a life or death decision, so don't let it hold you back from taking action. You can always change your theme later and even kill off your blog entirely if you get traction in another direction. The key is to get started. Good things NEVER come from sitting around and waiting. Good things come to those who take action.

Carve out an hour for yourself and make a list of topics. Then, write or record. In fact, most successful bloggers will tell you to **create content in chunks**, meaning when you're feeling inspired, knock out three or four blogs so you've got something stored in the pantry.

Keep your content value-based. This is not the boiler room sales hour. If you only blog about your business and/or products, you are missing out on a large slice of the pie.

As we've talked about, roughly 3% or less of the population is actively looking for what you have. A blog is a fantastic way to get the attention of the other 97% so you will be ready when they are.

Choose a web service and domain name

There are plenty of free websites out there to get you started. WordPress, ProBlogger, and Weebly all offer a free version. Free often means limited features, no domain name, and there's a possibility of ads on your blog that you cannot control. I encourage you to reach out to people you trust and ask what service they use and why they like it.

There is NOTHING wrong with using a free service to get started, especially if you aren't 100% sure about your topics or how you will promote your work. However, if you are really serious about this, as I mentioned before, I suggest making a commitment to purchase a domain name, which most free websites offer as a paid, add-on service. When you give out the domain name AlexTheis.com or StopPitching.com it is memorable and shows your commitment. When your blog's address is FreeBlogService.com/AlexTheis it can be confusing or hard to remember.

While there is nothing wrong with getting started with a free website to hose your blog, I encourage you to look at the pros and cons of paid web hosting. The subject of building a website, from choosing a domain name to developing your site could be an entire book by itself. I am not going to go into website development in this book, but know that there is a plethora of information about website creation available online.

The extra step and cost of having a web designer create and maintain your site is not necessary, but is a viable option. If you do this, don't overpay for heaven's sake!!! Use someone reputable, preferably a recommendation from someone you trust.

In addition, if you have a designer create your website, make sure you are able to upload and maintain content easily. You NEVER want to rely on your web designer to post blogs for you. This is a recipe for failure.

Wait a second – you are going to create a podcast or upload your videos to YouTube or Vimeo, so you think you don't need a website? Please reconsider. Even if you aren't producing a written blog online, make sure you create a website so people can see what you're about, download any support tools or info products you create (more on these later), and **connect** with you.

Find out what will work for you and persevere. **Make it happen!**

Learn the technology

Even though posting blogs, writing material, or recording won't take tons of time, you do need to invest some time in learning new technology if you don't know it already.

Get some help if you need it. This does not have to cost you money. Use Google to find training on setting up your website. There are so many great videos and tutorials out there! I promise you will get the help you need. You can also ask someone you know to train you on using your site, editing software, or any other new technology you want to take on.

POST! Be maniacally consistent.

Yes, I'm being repetitive. But it bears repeating. You will impact your personal brand online if you don't take this seriously. Be consistent in your posting and do it for the long haul. Make a commitment for the next 12 months and stick with it.

"There is no secret formula….the key is being consistent…if you're consistent in your posting and staying connected, you will always be ahead of the curve," says Luke Dancy.

Promote, share

Once you've written a blog or recorded a video and posted it to your website the fun begins - promoting your messages to the world.

"Social media is a must for a blog," says Lisha Yost. "Personally, Twitter is my favorite site for getting traffic to a blog because it's very information focused. **I get 30% of my traffic from Twitter.** My strategy is to tweet often (but not too often). I tweet my own blog posts of course, but I also tweet other similar blogs too, so my followers can benefit from information they're providing as well."

She continues, "You can't just write words and hope people will see them, not to mention like them. You need to get people to know your website exists, get them to come, and get them to want to come back for more."

Here's where your social media strategy kicks in. I want your new masterpiece to help you connect with people. So you need to make sure you are posting on your preferred social media channel(s) regularly. Not just links to your blogs or videos! Remember the 80/20 rule or even a 90/10 rule when promoting your blog.

Spread the word about your blog intertwined in your daily posts and tweets. Make it a part of your daily routine, but in a way that adds value, not a pitching, selling, or annoying way.

Cliff Ravenscraft advises, "Genuinely get in and connect with people. Build relationships with people who share your passion. Network with other bloggers who blog about the topic. Build relationships with other podcasters."

Here's where you can ask for help. You've got a built-in fan club already, right? I'm talking about your friends, family, co-workers, and associates.

Start on Facebook by telling everyone you have a new blog. Invite friends to comment on it or send you an email with their feedback. Ask people what they would like to see on your blog.

Now, reach out to people you trust via email. Select a handful of people who have your best interests at heart and want to see you succeed. Send them a short email message informing them about your new blog. Ask them to read it and subscribe, and if they like it, ask them to tell someone about it.

I've found through experience that people may read your blog and genuinely like it, but they may not spread the word or subscribe unless you ask them to. They get busy. They forget. No big deal.

Remember, do not ask in a pushy way. Ask it as a favor. Most of us have a limited number of favors available, so discern who you can ask.

The key is to find a promoting formula that's not too heavy, but still gets the word out. I'm often surprised when someone tweets me thanking me for my blog or a certain message. I never knew they read it. They are not subscribed. Here's a chance to ask for help. If someone likes your work and comments, simply reply and ask them to tell a friend.

Part of your promoting and social media strategy MUST include promoting other people, other businesses, and other blogs. By doing this in a genuine way, you will get other people promoting you and your message.

Keep a schedule and write in spurts

I've already mentioned that most bloggers I know will write or create content in chunks. Others will specifically schedule time to develop material. I do both. I will set aside 30 minutes to write a blog, post it, and schedule promotion.

If I'm feeling inspired, I can get two, three, or four blogs done during this time or at least make a list of other blogs I want to write when I have time.

To be consistent, your blog work needs to be a habit. Habits get created through routines and schedules. Make it a priority and you will get it done. Make excuses and your dreams may never come true.

Highly recommended reading: *The War of Art* by Steven Pressfield and *The Compound Effect* by Darren Hardy.

Subscribe and learn – be a student of the game

This is self-explanatory. If you want to grow as a social media user and blogger, be student of the game. Read other blogs. Listen to podcasts. Be a subscriber. Set aside 30 minutes a week to learn something new about social media. Read a chapter a day about blogging or online marketing. You're already doing it by reading this book. Keep going!

Even more recommended reading: *Platform* by Michael Hyatt. Not just for blogging. This is a manual for creating your online brand.

"Every business (or entrepreneur) should have a blog and publish a relevant post once a week or once a month (or more if possible). People who want a place to talk about anything they want should have a blog," says Lisha Yost.

Like Nike says, "Just do it." It's time. If you've been yearning to start that blog or you can feel it in your bones that this is for you, get started. There is no reason why you can't have something up and running in the next seven days.

APPLICATION:

1. Now that you've been able to brainstorm topics, ideas, and format (writing, audio, or video) for your blog, it's time to get started. Pick your format and start creating. Don't wait.

2. To start a free blog or website, go to Google and find services you can use without being charged.
3. Be sure to get a domain name for your site. Your custom address shows that you're serious.
4. Using a paid service for your website? Do your research. Ask a few people what they use and make an informed decision.
5. Remember that social networking, including blogging, is just one area of a well-rounded marketing strategy for your business. Make time each week for follow up phone calls, texts, and face-to-face meetings.

SECTION 8: PUTTING IT ALL TOGETHER

"I would love to have you on my show to talk about your book," the entrepreneur with the podcast interview show wrote me in an email.

"I love what you're up to. If there's a chance for us to work together on a project, I would like to discuss it more," the former professional athlete told me over the phone.

"Does it make sense for us to take our conversation offline? There may be an opportunity here," the life coach from Australia wrote to me on Twitter.

These are just a few of the times my online presence led to offline connections. You see my friends, the ultimate goal of the Stop Pitching, Start Connecting strategy is to put you in position for the right people to find you. Following this strategy, it's happened to me over and over, and it can happen to you too.

Meeting new people online, through social networking, has been nothing short of magical for me. A source of inspiration and motivation that excites me every single day. I know, through personal experience, that some percentage of these virtual meetings will eventually be taken offline through a Skype session, phone call, or a face-to-face meeting.

Recently, I connected with someone on Twitter who started a podcast that became popular very, very quickly. I simply reached out and said, "Congrats on the success of your podcast. I'd love to know how you did it. If you're open to a quick call, I'd like to ask you just a couple questions." I wasn't sure what to expect. Much to my surprise, within a few minutes, he replied. "I'm free for the next 30 minutes if you're able to talk."

He answered all of my questions, gave me valuable advice, and offered to help me anytime I had challenges in the future. What did I do to deserve this incredible mentoring? Simple. I was myself. No pitching. No spamming. No hidden agenda. Perhaps the greatest validation came as we opened our call and I thanked him. He said, "I'm happy to talk with

Alex. I see what you're up to. You're legit. You're trying to help people, so I want to help you."

BOOM!

As you read this final section, know that as you put it all together you are creating your future. New connections, fresh inspiration, and assistance from people who seemingly have nothing to gain from helping you. Believe it my friends. It will happen.

CHAPTER 36: IN-PERSON CONNECTIONS

How do I turn online relationships into personal relationships? That is the million dollar question. Here's where the rubber meets the road.

Trust the process

Trust that what you've learned will help you turn your online connections into real world relationships. Believe that if you implement the strategies in this book, you will inevitably meet new people in your town and throughout the world.

Bruce Van Horn says, "When it's done right, it really opens you up to more opportunities. The world has changed. People I have met over the last two years through social media, I've become closer friends with them than some of my neighbors. I have created true friendships through social media. Your market, people who may join your business, could be anywhere in the world."

Remember that I put this information together from personal experience. Many people I met through social media are now friends, associates, coaches, and partners outside of social networking channels.

This book is proof. Social media has not only helped me meet many of these great people, it has helped me strengthen my relationships with them after talking to them on the phone or meeting them in person.

It's easy to think, "How can this happen? How and when will I take online relationships offline?" These are the wrong areas of focus. Instead, create the vision. Focus on connecting and adding value to people. "Set the vision – your GPS. Then do the work. Do those two things and the 'how' will take care of itself," advises Dayne Gingrich.

Sometimes I sit in awe of the people who I've met online. I've been able to grow and deepen my connection with them on social media. People I would have never met otherwise have come into my life, some of them making a profound impact on me (and hopefully me on them).

Trust this process. It works. I'm living proof. Get excited about the possibilities. Expect good things to happen. Expect that in the next 12-18-24 months you are going to meet some incredible, like-minded people that you will work with in person or over the phone after meeting them through social networking.

Make connecting your only agenda

The only way I know to make sure your social media connections become in-person associations is to make **connecting** the only item on your agenda. If you are seeking to meet people offline for the sole purpose of having them buy from you, it won't work. I don't know how to put it any other way.

If connecting for the purpose of adding value and promoting others isn't your primary goal, this process will not work. In fact, it might work against you.

JB Glossinger has said many, many times on his CoachCast that he wants to have a million friends. Not a million customers. Not a million subscribers. Not a million prospects. Not a millions names in his marketing funnel. Nope. He legitimately wants one million friends. He knows that if he has a million friends that his value, process, funnel, strategy, and confidence will do the rest.

There have been times when I have really wanted someone to follow me. There were people I furthered my connection with on social media that I desperately wanted to work with. During those times, I found myself trying too hard. Promoting them so they would notice me. Retweeting them in hopes they would like me or seek me out.

None of that has ever worked. The only way it has worked for me is when my only agenda is to connect for the sake of connecting. Promote them because I love what they do. Retweet them because I got value from what they posted. Invited my friends on Facebook to use their services, buy their products, visit their website, etc., because I use their services, buy their products, and listen to their podcast.

Connect to connect and for no other reason, and good things will happen. I promise.

Meetups

Meetups happen in every town, state, and country. It's where like-minded people get together to network and connect. There are network marketing meetups. Business meetups. Speaker meetups. Crafting meetups. Mom meetups. Beer meetups. You get the picture. Meetups happen in person and online.

Find some meetups in your area and attend them. These could be networking events, trainings, or conferences. Find out where people like you and your target market are hanging out and put yourself there. Meetup.com is a great place to start.

Can't find a meetup or the right networking group? Start one yourself. I've been part of several of these, either starting them on my own or contributing to a group in its infancy. You can do it if you really want to.

When my large mastermind group wasn't meeting my needs, I started my own smaller group. It started with a weekly conference call and grew into an in-person event in Las Vegas.

Social media has made it easier than ever to grow your network and maintain communication. Whether it's meeting new people or keeping in touch with your team, social networking is here to make it more efficient and profitable.

Get people together. Online, on the phone, or in person. Lead by example.

Ask

If you really want to connect with someone and the opportunity hasn't made itself available, just ask.

I knew my 'connecting only' agenda was working when I got a direct message seemingly out of the blue on Twitter. It was someone I had connected with there who wanted to have a phone call with me. Their message simply said: "Looks like we have very similar businesses. Does it make sense for us to connect over the phone?"

This scenario has played itself out many times over. Sometimes it goes nowhere. Sometimes I get pitched (imagine that – boo!). Other times it has led to referrals and further networking opportunities. And still other times it's led directly to partnerships and business opportunities.

If you're serious about connecting with someone for mutual benefit or because you think you can help someone, just ask. That's what I did for this book. I simply asked people if I could tap into their expertise and opinions. And you know what? People said yes.

APPLICATION:

1. Trust the process. Who can you connect or reconnect with this week?
2. How will you adapt the **Stop Pitching and Start Connecting** strategy into your social media?
3. Check for meetups in your area. Attend one in the next 30 days. Remember, no agenda other than connecting. You may get pitched by others. That's okay. Stand out by connecting instead.

CHAPTER 37: IDEAS TO EXPAND YOUR NETWORK

None of the following ideas for tools, services, or products will take the place of prospecting, connecting, or following up. This book is NOT designed to allow you to stay home all day and collect checks. This book is only for the social media part of your platform and marketing strategy.

To be a success in business it takes more than just social media, blogging, or information products. However, all of these can add greatly to your warm market pipeline and lead generation.

Ideas – How can I get more names, contacts, prospects, and connections?

Think about a funnel. The wider it is, the more it collects, the more it collects, the more that can reach the bottom of the funnel. Let's widen your marketing funnel.

When you think about ideas to gain more connections, think big picture. Remember the 97% and don't just go after the 3%. Think of ideas you can implement that will be fun, ignite your passion, tap into your expertise, and attract a larger group of your target, or future target market.

I'm a big fan of creating tools, services, and products that articulate your expertise, help people, and return results in the form of fans, subscribers, and contacts. It's all about adding value.

Here's a list to get your brainstorming started. Be a student of the game as you come up with ideas. See what's working in the world, what you like, and what you can make your own.

Teleclasses/teleseminars

No matter what you call them – conference calls, teleclasses, or teleseminars – these are an easy way to invite people to find out who you are. Teleclasses are simply a call that you invite people to tune into. You can hold them live, record them, and make them available later, or use them as a way to create a podcast.

Here's an example:

Let's say you're really passionate about homeschooling. You can hold a teleclass that teaches people the do's and do not's of homeschooling. You could create a series of these calls, educating on a different aspect of homeschooling each time.

Your first call could be called, "Why homeschooling works in today's society," or, "The pros and cons of homeschooling your kids."

Your next call could be titled, "How to get started homeschooling. Is it right for your kids?"

Next, you could hold calls about homeschooling books and resources, how to work with your community, how to manage your time, and how to teach different age groups and grade levels.

As you hold these calls on a regular basis, you could create a cycle of 4-10 (or more) classes that you then repeat over and over. As people gain value and tap into your expertise, they trust you.

How does this help your business? Glad you asked.

First, you passively include your opportunity or products in your teleclasses. You don't pitch your products or educate people on them, you create curiosity instead.

Next, create a case or need for your opportunity or products, again, passively, through your stories and teachings.

Once you have developed trust and people are loving the value you are giving away, provide a few irresistible offers. At the end of your teleclass, you say something like this: "If you like what you heard tonight, here's a few ways you can get more of what we offer."

"First, our classes are 100% free and always will be. So tune in anytime, and invite a friend. Next, we mentioned some of the products we use with our kids. Our homeschooling seminar is ending, so if you would like to hear more about these outstanding products and how we make money working from home, stick around for the next 10 minutes. If not, we love ya and hope to hear you next week."

See how my offer is still opt-in, no pitching? Most people will jump off the call at this point, but they will leave without feeling like they got sold or pushed on. This is a big deal. If they feel safe, they will come back and/or invite their friends.

On the flipside, if you've delivered great content, been engaging, and developed trust, someone will stick around to hear about your exciting products or offer. Now, here's where you can make your pitch! Keep it short, simple, and packed with value. Then, make an offer to these people who are interested.

See how our connecting agenda can win over people and give you golden opportunities? Building trust creates opportunities.

The teleclass model can work well because people can tune in almost anywhere and hear the recording later if they miss it.

One of the keys is to find a way to passively introduce what you have to offer. If you use your creativity, and I know you're packed with it, you will find way.

I'll give you one more example:

Let's say I offered teleclasses on how to brew beer. How could I passively present my products or business? Simple. Brewing beer takes time. Time is a commodity for most people. If people are loving my brewing education but struggle with finding time to brew, I mention that.

"I know many of you struggle finding time to brew. That's why I recommend finding a way to work more from home, get more time off, or have more flexible work hours. I know a flexible schedule has made it much easier for me to brew when I want to."

So I set the stage, then at the end of the call I make an offer for people to hear more about how I get flexible hours and how they can too.

Webinars

Webinars are very similar to teleseminars/conference calls, but they have the addition of a visual component. Your audience not only gets to hear you talk, but they see your computer screen. This requires you creating visuals, usually through PowerPoint or a similar program. It also means that your guests must be in front of a computer on the internet or be able to access data at fast speeds on their smartphone.

One of the great things about webinars is being able to tap into visual learners. You can also record webinars for playback later.

The cons of a webinar are that they rely heavily on connectivity and are prone to have glitches. Because your audience is required to see what you're presenting, it's almost impossible to participate if you are not at home or in a stationary place with your computer or phone. You certainly cannot tune into a webinar while driving a car.

A lot of what you choose depends on what you like using. If you hate creating visuals, then try a conference call/teleclass. If you are a visual learner, producing webinars may be for you.

With a webinar, you can use the same format for making your opt-in offer at the end.

It's all about delivering outstanding value, engaging, connecting, and building trust. I know I sound like a broken record, but I cannot stress it enough.

It doesn't matter what you choose as a tool to help people get into your funnel – blogs, podcasts, videos, teleclasses, webinars, chats, etc. –

without being consistent you won't get the results you're looking for. If you give up too soon, you'll never get where you want to go.

Tweetchats

In the Twitter section of this book I went into Tweetchats quite heavily, mostly the benefits and how to join one. I placed it here to remind you that you can also host a Tweetchat.

Hosting a Tweetchat is only for those who get very versed on Twitter and gain a nice following. To make it work, you need to be very passionate about them and Twitter.

These may take considerably more time to get off the ground and gain an audience than webinars or teleclasses. Please understand I am not trying to talk you out of starting one, just want to make sure it's really for you and you're NOT wasting your time.

Infoproducts

Infoproducts, short for information products, are products you create with information and/or education. Very similar to a blog or video, except infoproducts include ebooks, white papers, manuals, workbooks, how-to guides, etc.

The difference between an infoproduct and a written blog is how they are delivered and what the consumer is required to do to receive them.

In *Book Yourself Solid*, author Michael Port raves about the power of infoproducts. I highly recommend checking out his book if you're interested in growing your personal brand.

Consider infoproducts not as something you do instead of a blog, video, teleclass, etc., but something that works in conjunction with these other social tools.

An example:

If I have a blog about clean eating, I offer free videos on how to shop for and prepare food for this lifestyle. I start generating an audience. When I want to capture *even more* contact details and add people to my database, I can create an infoproduct.

My infoproduct could be a free ebook that is a step-by-step manual to accompany my videos. In order to receive my free ebook, I would ask visitors to give me their email address. When people trust you and want more of what you provide, they will gladly give you their email address to download your 10-page ebook on clean eating.

There is also an opportunity to charge for really good infoproducts, especially if you put together a good sized ebook, audio program, or video series. I do not want to distract you from your core business. You are a networker. Don't derail yourself and lose leader support by putting your eggs in too many baskets.

Focus on one information product to start. Something that can help you gain more and more contacts. Do this for the sole purpose of making more connections, not making sales.

I heard a great story about a small time barbeque chef who started a blog. He blogged about his recipes and catering. To get more subscribers to his blog, he created a short ebook with his best recipes. The book was free, all you had to do to download it was provide this cook with your email address. After months of providing his best recipes for free, he started to email market to his THOUSANDS of addresses he collected. By doing the work once – a short ebook of recipes – this cook bought time to put together a much more robust cookbook.

When he was ready to launch his new cookbook for $19.95, guess where his greatest marketing success happened? That's right, through the people who already loved this chef because he gave them great value. The people who downloaded his original ebook for free were the top purchasers of his new book.

Your information product can work just as well. Don't rush it, though. I've thrown a lot at you in this book. Big picture is still a long-term, marathon approach. You need a strategy.

If you go out and create a terrific information product tomorrow, but have no online platform, no social media presence, and no website to collect names and email addresses, you may get discouraged quickly.

Infoproducts can happen literally overnight. An ebook can be as simple as a collection of your best blogs. It's really that simple.

Never, never, never, ever let the creation of information products get in the way of working your business. Excuses and time wasters get you nowhere.

APPLICATION:

1. Do some research on information products. Experience a webinar or download a free ebook. What format can you see yourself creating in the future?
2. Take a few minutes and write down ideas for infoproducts you could create, including topics and formats.
3. If now isn't the time to create an infoproduct, come back to this chapter later. When the time comes, you can brainstorm ideas to develop something you're proud of.
4. Infoproducts are not limited to what we covered in this chapter. You could create online courses, DVDs, audio programs, or something that's never been done before! Sometimes the best product to create is the one you can't find out there, something that you would use but doesn't exist.

CHAPTER 38: PUTTING IT ALL TOGETHER

Congratulations. You've made it this far. You're committed to your social media success. You believe in yourself and your ability to develop your personal brand online. I believe in you too.

Everything in this book is meant to be a supplement to your business, not be your business. Keep that in mind.

Social networking is not complicated. There is no magic bullet. Success is simply a process of strategy – consistency, content, a marathon approach, learning, and an over-arching theme of connecting above all else.

If you do nothing else in this book, stop pitching and start connecting. If you weren't pitching and selling – awesome. Still, do more connecting anyway. I promise if you make connecting your top agenda item, great things will happen.

The benefits of using social media effectively as an entrepreneur and business owner cannot be measured. It will take time, but if you're willing to stick to the plan, trust the process, and follow the strategy, you will win. Open your mind to the possibilities.

Here is where we separate the wishers from the doers. Those who succeed from those who don't try. If you are diligent, social media will open up doors you never knew existed. You will develop fulfilling relationships, endless referrals, and a new way to expand your warm market like never before.

In any type of sales, lead generation is pivotal. For years I've heard network marketers complain about running out of people to talk to. Then they discover social media, only to spoil it by pitching, promoting, and chasing away people who may very well be interested one day. But not you.

Now you see that if you put in the work, you have a new source of leads. A clean, fun, genuine source to tap into word-of-mouth advertising like never before. New ways to attract people into your funnel. Blogs. Twitter. Infoproducts. Pinterest. Podcasts. YouTube. The list keeps growing.

"Social media opens doors and creates relationships that otherwise just wouldn't happen. It's easier and easier to meet the right people as long as you carry yourself the right way and know what you're doing." –Luke Dancy

Here's the separation factor: are you willing to put this book into action?

Those who take action will forge a new course for their future. They will learn and grow and add to their network every day. They will stick with it, even when there's a speed bump or an obstacle. Using the foundation in this book, they will create their own strategy, and build teams of people who look up to them.

Will this be you? Make it happen.

The best advice, education, or instruction is useless without action. Start today. Don't wait. Begin slowly if you want. It's okay. Be the tortoise. Slow and steady. Win this race.

Listen to the advice of the fantastic experts in this book. They are living it. I am living it—and loving it! Social media has added value to my life, both professionally and personally.

I want to add one last story to prove the power of social media.

As I write this, just yesterday I had a meeting with Chef Oz, who is quoted in this book. It was a casual meeting, a celebration of sorts after his appearance on *Cutthroat Kitchen*. Here he was, a budding celebrity, sitting with me and my wife on a Monday afternoon. When I met Oz, he was a restaurateur with even bigger dreams. Now those dreams are starting to come to fruition.

Talk about friends in high places. Oz is growing his network and connecting, constantly. He's the epitome of the 90/10 rule and a great example of the stop pitching, start connecting strategy. The food at his restaurant is great, but people come for more than that.

They come to be welcomed by Oz. They stop in because of the way they feel when they are there. The service they get. The experience. It's everything – the food, the drink, the people. But mostly, it's the owner and how he treats people. No agenda, no pitching, just connecting and being human.

Oz has introduced me to many people, one of which I came very close to joining on a very big business deal. Others have become friends. That's the referability that Steve Gutzler talks about. I connected with Oz. Built trust. Promoted him. Likewise, he returned the favor. We've enjoyed meals, coffee, and hikes together.

Oz is more than someone I follow or a Facebook friend. He's like a brother. Those types of relationships are very hard to come by.

Where did I meet Oz? On *Twitter*.

I met Oz on social media. He lives in my town, but it took social media for me to get connected with him. We were friends for months on Twitter before we ever met in person.

The power of social media cannot be measured, my friends. Believe it. When used in the right way, it will help you find people you never would have met otherwise.

All it takes is a little bit of your time and a solid strategy. Not rocket science. No secret formula. No magic bullet. Be yourself and connect with people.

The world could always use more greatness.

Stay hungry and start today. You *can* do this. I'm right behind you.

RESOURCES AND GIFTS - FOR YOU

As a special gift to you, I have put together all of my interviews into an ebook of their own. This compilation of interviews with social media and business leaders is available to you, absolutely free, by going to: StopPitching.com/Resources. Just fill out the quick form and your FREE ebook will be on its way to your inbox.

You can also visit StopPitching.com/Resources to find a growing selection of free tools and resources to help you create your winning social media strategy, including the Strategy Session Guide, Blogging Worksheet, Expo Tips and Strategy Guide, and an article I wrote for *Raine Magazine* about online marketing for entrepreneurs like you. In addition, here are books, blogs, podcasts, and other resources I recommend:

Books:

- *The Pinterest Diet: How to Pin Your Way Thin* by Mitzi Dulan
- *Pinterest Tutorial: Pinterest Help for Beginners* by Michelle Held
- *Platform* by Michael Hyatt
- *The War of Art* by Steven Pressfield
- *Advertising Headlines That Make You Rich* by David Garfinkel
- *The Compound Effect* by Darren Hardy
- *The Barefoot Executive* by Carrie Wilkerson
- *Go For No* by Richard Fenton and Andrea Waltz

Blogs:

- SevenSentences.com (Geoff Talbot)
- BlogandRetire.com (Lisha Yost)
- ChrisFreytag.com (Chris Freytag)
- NutritionExpert.com (Mitzi Dulan)
- BeachBoundBooks.com (Stacie Theis)
- MichaelHyatt.com (Michael Hyatt)

Podcasts:

- MorningCoach.com (JB Glossinger)
- Life Is A Marathon (Bruce Van Horn)
- PodcastLimitless.com (Alex Theis)
- Joel Osteen's audio podcast – on iTunes

WILL YOU HELP ME?

If you enjoyed any part of Stop Pitching & Start Connecting, would you mind taking a minute to write a review on Amazon? Even a short review really helps, and it would mean a lot to me.

If you know someone who is struggling with social media or could use some ideas to expand their engagement and reach through social networking, please send them a copy of this book or refer them to it on Amazon. I want to help as many people as possible grow their personal brand and feel confident about staking their claim on social media.

If you would like to order bulk copies of this book for your team, organization, or company, please contact me via email at: Info@StopPitching.com. I offer bulk discounts and free books when I speak for your group.

Lastly, to check out more about this book, future books, and updates on my upcoming projects, visit StopPitching.com.

Thank you,

Alex Theis

CONNECT WITH ME

I want to hear from you! Let's connect.

You can follow me on Twitter (@AlexTheis) and check out my blog at StopPitching.com.

If you're interested in joining any of my workshops, group coaching sessions, mastermind groups, laser coaching sessions, or if you would like one-on-one coaching, visit StopPitching.com/Coaching and request a custom quote.

To book me as your next speaker or trainer or to work with me on your company's social media strategy, visit my Speaking or Services page at StopPitching.com.

For all other services or inquiries, please contact me at StopPitching.com or email me: Alex@StopPitching.com.

Thank you for taking the time to read this book. I hope you will take a minute to send me a note on Twitter or email.

Happy connecting!

THE EXPERTS FEATURED IN THIS BOOK

The people I interviewed are the real deal. They are using social media every day to connect and grow their warm market. Each of them epitomizes the *Stop Pitching & Start Connecting* strategy. Please take a moment to follow them on Twitter, check out their podcasts, videos, written blogs, website, or books. You'll be glad you did.

(Listed in alphabetical order by last name)

LYDIA ASWOLF-CAREY

LydiaAswolf.com/blog/

Twitter: @LydiaAswolf

Lydia is a book reviewer, blogger, and social media brand manager. She uses social media to connect and get more customers by powerful word of mouth. Lydia has a solid grasp on what works in social networking and has a well-rounded resume of experience with many different social media challenges. She has worked with many different companies and brands to improve their social media engagement. She is also a regular contributor to *VividLifeUK*.

OSVALDO BLACKALLER (CHEF OZ)

CuevaBar.com

Twitter: @CuevaBar

Chef Oz has a remarkable story. On his drive home after being laid off from his corporate job, he spotted a space for lease. His dream had always been to open his own place. He had no formal culinary training, no business ownership experience, and very little capital. He's proof that when you want something badly enough, you can make it happen. His restaurant, called Cueva Bar, is now a successful fixture in the University Heights/North Park communities of San Diego. Chef Oz uses social media to communicate with his customers, spread the word about his awesome food, and meet people in San Diego he wouldn't meet otherwise.

Chef Oz recently appeared on the Food Network show *Cutthroat Kitchen*.

BK BOREYKO

Twitter: @BKBoreyko

BK is one of my greatest mentors. It was a great experience to interview him and hear his insights. He's a straight shooter, a risk taker, and a competitive yet heart-based business owner and leader. He has over twenty years of experience in the wellness and network marketing industries, as both a distributor and an owner of multi-million dollar companies he founded. In 2004 he launched a new company, a launch I had the privilege of being involved in. BK thinks like a distributor first and an owner/executive second, and I have always admired him for that. He taught me the value and benefits of entrepreneurship and how to get ahead by helping others get ahead.

DAVID COLISTER

www.DavidColister.com

Twitter: @Colister

David is a network marketing and direct sales professional – an MLM philosopher as he calls it. His work has been the catalyst for billions of dollars in sales with several large companies in the direct sales industry.

David is a personal friend and mentor of mine who has helped me grow immensely over the years.

I believe David's greatest traits are the way he truly cares about people, builds trust, and freely gives away all of his expertise and knowledge. He is another great example that if you make connecting your top agenda item, the business will follow.

BILL CORTRIGHT

EliteFitForever.com

Twitter: @BillCortright

Bill is a speaker, author, entrepreneur, coach, and personal trainer who has grown his network and business opportunities through social media. He is a leader in the field of stress management. His latest book is titled, *The Stress Response Diet and Lifestyle Program*. He is also the creator of the ground-breaking approach to total health and weight loss called *The BioFit Program*.

LUKE DANCY

LukeDancy.com and SocialMischief.net

Twitter: @LukeDancy

Luke is a professional magician and was a creator and consultant on the hit shows *Criss Angel: Mindfreak* and *Criss Angel: Believe*. He is an entrepreneur, speaker, blogger, and social media consultant and strategist. He is the founder of Social Mischief, a brand consulting, marketing, advertising, and social media strategy company whose clients have included the A&E Network, Spike TV, Cirque du Soleil, and Criss Angel.

LOLLY DASKAL

LollyDaskal.com

Twitter: @LollyDaskal

Lolly is the founder of Lead From Within, a global consultancy firm that offers custom programs in leadership and organizational development centered on heart-based leadership. She is an accomplished speaker, consultant, author, and facilitator. She was named in the Top 100 Leaders to Follow on Twitter by *The Huffington Post*, among other accolades.

Lolly also started the TwitterChat #leadfromwithin, which takes place every Tuesday at 5:00pm Pacific/8:00pm Eastern Time. Her TwitterChat has grown to include 4.5 million people every Tuesday evening.

MITZI DULAN

NutritionExpert.com

Twitter: @NutritionExpert

Mitzi is known as America's Nutrition Expert – a nationally recognized nutrition and wellness expert and author of the books *The Pinterest Diet: How to Pin Your Way Thin* and *The All-Pro Diet: Lose Fat, Build Muscle, and Live Like a Champion*, which she wrote with future NFL Hall of Famer Tony Gonzalez, who played for the Kansas City Chiefs and Atlanta Falcons.

Mitzi is currently the team nutritionist for Major League Baseball's Kansas City Royals, and formerly worked with the NFL's Kansas City Chiefs, the NBA's Golden State Warriors, and the NHL's San Jose Sharks. She has regularly been seen on Fox News Channel, *Live! With Kelly and Michael*, *The Dr. Oz Show*, and CNN.

She was named one of the Top 20 Nutrition Experts to Follow on Twitter by *The Huffington Post* and has a very engaged social media audience with over 3.7 million Pinterest followers.

TRACEY EHMAN

WomenSpeakersAssociation.com

Twitter: @PartnerInBiz

Tracey is an online presence and social media strategist who focuses on creating a cohesive and targeted presence across all social media platforms, including websites, for her clients. She believes that you need to show up online, in the same way you would show up in person. Tracey is also an Honorary Founding partner of the Women Speakers Association, responsible for the first rendition of the website, and manager of social media.

Tracey co-hosts the TwitterChat #SpeakerChat every Tuesday at 4:00pm PT

CHRIS FREYTAG

ChrisFreytag.com

Twitter: @ChrisFreytag

Chris is a national health and wellness expert, author, fitness trainer and fitness personality. For the last twenty years she has been a certified fitness trainer, certified health coach, and regular contributor to many different health, fitness, and business publications, including *Prevention* and *Success*. One of her top priorities is to help people cut through the confusion and get healthy. She has appeared on multiple radio and television shows as well, including being a regular personality on the QVC Network.

LAUREN GALLEY

GirlsAboveSociety.org

Twitter: @LaurenMGalley

Lauren is the Founder and President of Girls Above Society, a non-profit organization that empowers tween and teen girls to become confident leaders, while maintaining positive values as they face the pressures of today's society. Lauren is also an accomplished speaker, author, mentor, model, and actress. She has used social media to expand her network, spread the news about her organization, and mentor others. She hosts *The Lauren Galley Show* on CETV, is a regular contributor to *The Huffington Post*, and wrote the book *Girls Above Society - Steps to Success: An Empowerment Guide* – a confidence and empowerment guide for teen girls.

DAYNE GINGRICH

CoachDayne.com

Twitter: @CoachDayne

Dayne is a former professional athlete turned coach. He works with high performers to develop a 1% mindset. With a driving force to help others live a life of confidence and passion, all of his coaching is aimed at eliminating the acceptance of mediocrity and elevating expectations for what we can achieve. He specializes in helping people overcome a fear-based mentality so they can boldly go after their dreams.

JB GLOSSINGER

MorningCoach.com

Twitter: @MorningCoach

JB is a podcaster and leader in the world of new ideas, fresh thought, and the founder of personal evolution through his Morning Coach podcast. He has been a mentor of mine for several years. His 'CoachCast' as it's called has listeners in more than 100 countries and is regularly one of the top podcasts on iTunes. He recently celebrated his 2000th CoachCast.

JB is also a speaker, author, and coach, with an MBA and PhD in Metaphysics.

STEVE GUTZLER

SteveGutzler.com

Twitter: @SteveGutzler

Steve is the President of Leadership Quest, a Seattle, Washington based leadership development company. Steve is a speaker and coach whose clients include Microsoft, Starbucks, Boeing, Cisco, Starwood, and the Seattle Seahawks. He is the author of the book *Emotional Intelligence for Personal Leadership* and was voted the Most Inspirational Leader on Social Media by readers of *The Huffington Post*.

MICHELLE HELD

MetroNY.com

Twitter: @MetroNY

Michelle is the author of the book *Pinterest Tutorial: Pinterest Help for Beginners*. She is an entrepreneur that works with organizations to develop an overall marketing strategy from management, IT, and public relations. Michelle manages and produces content for her clients' official presence on targeted social media and traditional platforms to ensure it aligns with their overall business strategy. Her specialty is working with the nonprofit sector.

JARED MCMULLIN

FridayNightCranks.com

Twitter: @FNC

Jared is the founder of Friday Night Cranks, a live comedy/prank call webcast that takes place every Friday at 6:00pm Pacific Time. He also runs the popular Friday Night Cranks YouTube channel, producing and hosting videos with multimillion views.

CLIFF RAVENSCRAFT

PodcastAnswerMan.com

Twitter: @GSPN

Cliff Ravenscraft is the founder of the Generally Speaking Production Network. Together with his wife and a few close friends, Cliff has produced over 3,200 podcast episodes, since December 2005, devoted to Entertainment, Family, Faith, Fitness, Career and Technology.

Cliff has helped thousands of people launch successful podcasts through his *Podcasting A to Z* online training course. In the top 100 business podcasts on iTunes, more than 50 of these shows were created by Cliff's clients.

STEPHEN SHAPIRO

StephenShapiro.com

Twitter: @StephenShapiro

Stephen is one the world's leading authorities on innovation. He is a best-selling author, keynote speaker, advisor, and consultant on innovation. His clients include Microsoft, NASA, Staples, 3M, and Nike, just to name a few. His work has been features in *Forbes, The Harvard Business Review, The Wall Street Journal, ABC News*, and many other media outlets.

While I didn't specifically interview Stephen for the book, his insights are mentioned and his impression on me can be felt throughout several chapters.

JAMIE STEWART

MomentumFactor.co.uk/

Twitter: @MrJamie_Stewart

Jamie is the Managing Director of Momentum Factor Europe Ltd., a full service social media management and strategy company supporting businesses to realize their marketing goals and objectives. I consider Jamie both a peer and friend.

Before joining Momentum Factor, Jamie engineered a turnaround as the Managing Director of Kleeneze, one of the leading direct sales/network marketing companies in the United Kingdom. He also served as the Chairman of the Direct Selling Association UK.

Jamie is the epitome of the Stop Pitching, Start Connecting strategy. He understands that social media has allowed people to connect like never before and teaches people how to use social networking effectively every day.

GEOFF TALBOT

SevenSentences.com

Twitter: @GeoffTalbot

Geoff is the founder of a blog called Seven Sentences, which provides inspiration for creative people. He also consults, advises, and coaches businesses and entrepreneurs on finding their voice and creating a marketing strategy around that voice.

STACIE THEIS

BeachBoundBooks.com

Twitter: @BeachBoundBooks

Stacie is an entrepreneur, book reviewer, author, interviewer, and blogger. She started Beach Bound Books to help promote authors and their books. She has been a work-from-home mom since 1997 and has started several home-based businesses in the last 15 years, including success with Avon and eBay.

BRUCE VAN HORN

BruceVanHorn.com

Twitter: @BruceVH

Bruce is a life coach, speaker, podcaster, and social media influencer. He went from 17 followers on Twitter to almost 300,000 followers in just two years. His personal motto is, "Life is a marathon, so let's train for it!" Bruce also launched a podcast that quickly gained thousands of subscribers throughout the world on iTunes. His insights and expertise can be found on his website and Twitter.

LISHA YOST

BlogandRetire.com or TwonderWoman.com

Twitter: @BlogandRetire

Lisha is a self-made entrepreneur who has become an expert in the fields of social media, web traffic, and creating income from blogging. She currently runs a social media management business called Twonder Woman and runs three blogs. Lisha is also the founder of Blog and Retire University.

ACKNOWLEDGMENTS

I have deep gratitude for so many people who contributed to this book in ways big and small.

I am indebted for life to Paula Moldenhauer for her countless hours of help on this book. She wasn't afraid to ask the challenging questions, cut material, or rearrange entire sections, all with the big picture in mind. God certainly was smiling on me when he prompted me to ask for her feedback on what I thought was a final draft.

The people who I interviewed for this book were simply amazing. You will never meet a more giving group of people. Thank you Lolly Daskal, JB Glossinger, Bill Cortright, Luke Dancy, Jamie Stewart, Osvaldo Blackaller, Lydia Aswolf-Carey, Geoff Talbot, Tracey Ehman, Lauren Galley, Lisha Yost, Chris Freytag, Mitzi Dulan, Steve Gutzler, Michelle Held, Jared McMullin, BK Boreyko, Cliff Ravenscraft, Bruce Van Horn, and the beautiful Stacie Theis (my wife).

Enormous thanks to Connie Whitesell. Coach Connie has believed in me through thick and thin. The world needs more people like her.

Thank you to Stephen Shapiro and Becca Atterberry for nudging me, telling me like it is, mentoring me, and most of all, just for being a friend.

Huge kudos to Joshua Sprague for helping me with the logistics of writing a book.

Anne Marie Duquette and Scott Mitchell also played a role in editing this book and for that I am very grateful to them.

To my mentors who probably have no idea how much they have contributed to my success through the years – Brian Altman, Darren Hardy, Michael Hyatt, JB Glossinger, Joel Osteen, Carrie Wilkerson, BK

Boreyko, Kevin Fournier, Peter Reilly, Jayson Arfmann, Seth Godin, and Mike Rabbitts.

And finally, thanks to Wayne Hillman for bringing me to San Diego and for trusting me to build the ultimate trust with his field. May he rest in peace and see that blueprint to a billion come true in heaven.

REFERENCES

[1] Pew Internet (http://pewinternet.org/Commentary/2012/March/Pew-Internet-Social-Networking-full-detail.aspx) and *The Huffington Post*

[2] http://www.pewinternet.org/2012/05/07/just-in-time-information-through-mobile-connections/